GEORGE & ROBERT STEPHENSON

NATIONAL RAILWAY MUSEUM, YORK
SCIENCE MUSEUM, LONDON

George & Robert Stephenson

Michael Robbins

LONDON: HER MAJESTY'S STATIONERY OFFICE

For my son, Michael James Gordon Robbins

AUTHOR'S NOTE

This is a new edition of a small book originally published in 1966 by the Oxford University Press. For this edition I have made a few amendments to bring the text, and particularly the bibliographical note, up to date; but I have not found it necessary to revise any of the judgments which I came to when the book was written.

The illustrations have been selected afresh, with the help of the National Railway Museum, York, and other sources, as noted on pages vii-viii. The letter on page 35 is quoted by permission of the Huntington Library, San Marino, California; that on pages 26–7 is from the Hulton MSS in the Lancashire Record Office, Preston, transcribed by Professor Jack Simmons.

M. R.

London SW19
7 September 1980

Crown copyright 1981
First published by HMSO, 1981

ISBN 0 11 290342 8

Contents

◆

List of illustrations

◆

All photographs held by the National Railway Museum, York, except no. 2 from the Institution of Civil Engineers, London, and cover portrait of George Stephenson from British Railways.

MAPS

FIGURE *page 17*

Cast Tram Rail, Surrey Iron Railway, 1803. Losh and Stephenson's Patent Cast Rail, 1816. Stephenson's Wrought Iron Rail, Liverpool & Manchester Railway, 1829 (from C. E. Lee, *The Evolution of Railways*)

1
Britain on the eve of the Railway Age

◆

During the long war against revolutionary and imperial France which lasted, with two short intervals, from 1793 to 1815, Great Britain was still primarily an agricultural country; that is to say, more people were employed in agriculture than in any other activity, and, in general, the country fed itself without need of imports. The important towns were the old-established seaports–London, Plymouth, Bristol, Liverpool, Hull, Newcastle–or historic cities like York and Norwich, with a few growing centres of industry and trade, like Manchester for cotton and Birmingham for metal goods. The countryside was changing; the old 'unimproved' agricultural state, with wasteful farming in many parts of the country on great open tracts of land, was gradually being transformed into a pattern of neat, hedged fields farmed by better methods. Manufacturing industry was not, as it came to be in later years, normally carried on in towns; indeed, some of the most important industrial activities– coal-mining, iron-working, making cotton or woollen cloth, nails, stockings, gloves, chairs, and the like–were scattered about in villages. They were situated where their materials could be got locally, or, if mechanical power was required, where that could be obtained, converted either from the flow of water turning milling machinery or from coal through steam engines. Means of transport between the places where the ingredients of the industrial process– raw material and power–could be brought together and the markets where the goods could be sold were thus essential: transport was provided by roads, often poor in quality, sea transport, which supported a large coasting trade through a host of large and small ports, and inland waterways, primarily improved river channels or 'navigations', which since 1755 had been much extended in many parts of the country by artificial canals. Though the canals were of limited value as a national system, they had stimulated a great expansion of internal movement which had led to more efficient and productive manufacture. This growth in industrial ouput, combined with improvement in agriculture, enabled Britain to weather the long war with France and to support her continental allies without economic collapse.

But deficiency in internal transport was serious, and this remained the weakest link in the chain of production. In 1798 it took three nights and two days of hard travelling to get from London to Edinburgh; a few years earlier, it took thirty hours to Chester and another day on to Holyhead, for the sailing-packet to Ireland. For the transport of goods, canal boats moved at about $3\frac{1}{2}$ miles an hour if all went well; but frost in winter and lack of water in summer could stop all movement for days or weeks together. All carriage by land, either by road or canal, was expensive.

Coal was the leading, indeed the essential, product in Britain's economy. It was still in many places a luxury to burn for heating, but it was a necessity for the manufacture of iron and for the steam engines used for pumping and for driving machinery. If it was to have more than a purely local usefulness, the coal had to be moved from the pits to navigable water, either on a canal, as in Staffordshire, Lancashire, and parts of South Wales, or direct to a river estuary or to a seaport for coastwise shipping. In this respect, the coalfield in south Northumberland and north Durham enjoyed the splendid facility for shipping provided by the comparatively deep and sheltered mouth of the River Tyne; and London, in particular, had been supplied by coastal colliers from Tyneside since the Middle Ages. The pits from which the coal was dug were mainly situated in villages up to 10 miles from the water; and on Tyneside the skills of mining the coal and of transporting it, both underground and after it had been raised to the surface, were constantly being improved.

Wagon-ways, tramroads, railways—these were all variations of the parallel-rail method of facilitating the movement of wheeled vehicles.

2
George Stephenson, Engine-wright

◆

George Stephenson, second child of Robert Stephenson and his wife Mabel Carr, was born on 9 June 1781 in a small cottage which still stands on the edge of the village of Wylam, on the north bank of the Tyne some 8 miles above Newcastle. Old Robert earned 12s a week at his job of fireman of the Wylam colliery pumping engine, which kept the underground workings free from the water that always seeps into them. On this wage the family could keep respectable, but there was hardly any money for clothing, and none for schooling. George grew up a lively, active boy, knowledgeable about country things and observing the engines that his father tended and the horse-drawn wagon-ways by which the coal from the pits was led down to the Tyne for shipment. These wagon-ways were formed of two parallel lines of squared timber, kept in place by cross-pieces or ties; horses pulled 'chaldrons' or light wagons along them, each carrying about a ton, and fitted with flanges on their wheels to hold them on the rail-tops. The wagon-way was not normally laid straight on the surface of the ground but a comparatively level bed was fashioned for it by levelling off the minor bumps and hollows. The top surface of the rail was sometimes covered with a thin iron plate, to reduce wear. By these means, a horse could pull several chaldrons at one time.

The boy's first employment was watching cows and keeping them off the Dewley wagon-way for 2d a day; then he led horses at the plough, and hoed turnips for 4d a day. Next he became a 'picker', clearing out stones from coal, and after that driver of the gin-horse at Black Callerton, 2 miles from Dewley (a 'gin' was a drum or windlass for hoisting or pumping). When he was about fourteen, he went back to Dewley to help his father on the pumping engine. When that pit became exhausted, the family moved to a new pit, 'the Duke's Winning', belonging to the Duke of Northumberland, near Newburn; George became fireman at the Mid Hill Winning pit for 1s a day. This pit in turn was soon closed down, and he moved on to work an engine near Throckley Bridge; there his wages went up to 12s a week and he thought himself a man made for life. At seventeen he moved again—always 'following the work'—to Water Row, just west of Newburn, as plugman or engineman to a new engine erected by Robert Hawthorn, the duke's engineer; and his father became his fireman.

There, or in some such position in life, another man might have stuck; but George Stephenson's inborn curiosity, already excited by practical study of his engine, drove him on to learn reading and writing and then arithmetic at night-school, for which he paid first 3d and then 4d a week. Beginning in 1799, when he was eighteen, he studied hard and made progress. He mastered reading, but the act of writing was always a difficulty which he avoided if he could (in later life he had a secretary to write for him). He mastered arithmetic, but he could never perform a theoretical calculation.

From Water Row he went in 1801 to the Dolly Pit at Black Callerton as 'brakesman', which meant driving and controlling the winding mechanism which lifted the coal and the pitmen up the pit shaft in 'corves' or large wicker baskets. It was a fairly skilled job,

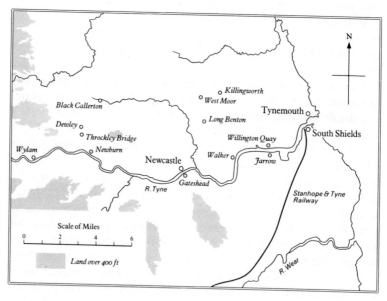

The Stephensons' Tyneside

rather monotonous with a good deal of spare time, which George was able to fill with writing and arithmetic (and mending shoes). At Black Callerton he stood up to insults from one Ned Nelson, the bully of the pit, took him on in a pitched fight with fists, and beat him. He was wiry and athletic and in good physical condition – he would have need of it.

So far all Stephenson's life had been spent within a few miles of his birthplace, at different collieries on the north or Northumberland side of the Tyne above Newcastle. His next move was to Willington Quay, on the eastern side of Newcastle about half-way to the sea at Tynemouth, where he became brakesman of a newly-installed engine hauling wagons for another purpose connected with the coal trade. The coal ships returning unladen from London had to take on 'ballast' – any kind of heavy material – to keep them stable at sea; on arrival, the ballast had to be emptied out and deposited on the top of an enormous rubbish-shoot – the 'Ballast Hill'. He owed this appointment to Robert Hawthorn. He had been married on 28 November 1802 to Frances Henderson, daughter of a small farmer at Capheaton, in Newburn church, and the couple settled in a two-storey cottage on Willington Quay. Here on 16 October 1803 their only son, Robert Stephenson, was born.

At Willington George began to show more clearly the toughness of mind which was to make him one of the outstanding men of the nineteenth century. He began to struggle with the theory of machines, and to work, from mechanical models, on perpetual motion, a puzzle that has teased inventive minds throughout the ages. More profitably, he mended shoes and clocks.

Towards the end of 1804 the little Stephenson family moved again, this time to Killingworth, 7 miles north of Newcastle, where George became brakesman to the West Moor colliery engine. His wife died at Killingworth in 1806, soon after giving birth to a daughter, who did not long survive. Shortly after this, George went up, on foot, to Montrose in Scotland for a year, to superintend the working of a steam engine at a spinning mill; little Robert was left in the charge of a housekeeper. George managed to save some money (£28, it is said) in Scotland; but two misfortunes required all his savings to be spent soon after his return – an accident which blinded his father, and call-up for the militia which involved paying for a substitute. This seems to have been the one period in his life when he felt absolute despair, and he thought of emigrating to America, as his sister Anne had already done; but he overcame the black mood, partly, it appears, by resolving to secure for his son the advantages of education that he knew he himself could never acquire. So began an intensive training for the little boy which might have proved too much for anyone with a less sturdy mind, leading to an association which made the name of Stephenson famous. As this story will show, some of the most important works of George Stephenson were undertaken during the period when his son was associated with him, and it is not clear—it probably never will be—exactly how much was contributed by each of them to the result. George's great gifts were stubbornness of character in the face of obstacles, allied to an instinctive understanding of the elements of engineering that often proved to be more correct than the answers calculated by cleverer people. Robert, who had, in everyday dealings at least, a gentler character than his father, contributed to the partnership a soundly-based theoretical knowledge; without this, the older man's intuition would at times have led the partnership astray.

George's unmarried sister Eleanor joined him at Killingworth to keep the house and mother young Robert, who began to attend Long Benton village school as soon as he could walk. When he was twelve, he was sent to Dr Bruce's private school in Percy Street, Newcastle, a distance of 5 miles each way which he soon began to cover on a donkey. What Robert had learned at school during the day was gone over by both father and son at night; and between them the man and the boy constructed and accurately marked out a sundial which was fixed over their cottage door, dated 11 August 1816. Robert stayed at the Newcastle school from 1815 to 1819, while George modestly prospered and added more rooms to his home at West Moor. Eleanor Stephenson left to marry about 1819, and in 1820 George married Elizabeth Hindmarsh, who had apparently been his first love while he was at Black Callerton.

George's prosperity began with a chance that came his way in 1811. The pumping engine at the High Pit at Killingworth, sunk the year before by the 'Grand Allies' (Lord Strathmore, Sir Thomas Liddell, later Lord Ravensworth, and Mr Stuart Wortley, later Lord Wharncliffe, some of the greatest coalowners of the North-East), was not working well.

Stephenson saw what was wrong with its design and offered to put the defects right if he could have his own mates working with him. He succeeded, and was paid £10. This was not much, but his name was made in the neighbourhood, and he was soon promoted engine-wright at Killingworth, and then given charge of all the machinery in the Grand Allies' collieries, with £100 a year, a horse, and the right to work for other proprietors also, provided that he kept his employers' equipment in good order. So George Stephenson became something of a general practical consultant on steam-driven mining machinery in the area where its application was making most rapid progress. Independence of action, within limits, was being added to his equipment.

The steam engines at the pits were concerned primarily with pumping the workings free from water. Wagon-ways, both below and above ground, by which trams or chaldrons were moved along rails, had been familiar to Stephenson since his very earliest days at Wylam, and during this period of his career he introduced many detailed improvements in the tracks, switches, and crossings, which enabled networks of rails to supersede the older and cumbrous method of transport by sleds. Steam power for haulage was already being applied to transport within colliery areas, the power being transmitted by ropes hauled by stationary engines, both above and below ground. Three such engines—'Geordie', 'Bobby', and 'Jimmy'— were installed underground at Killingworth by Stephenson, with his son's assistance after he had left school.

Throughout this time Stephenson was often underground and in daily contact with the work of the pitmen. He knew the dangers arising from the flues of his engines (which were carried up to the surface to discharge into the open air) when they became overheated, and he knew that there were far too frequent accidents caused by explosions of gas ignited by lights in the colliery workings; these made many parts of the pits uneconomical as well as dangerous to work. A safe miner's lamp was badly wanted. This was a challenge to his ingenuity. Other minds were exercised on this problem at the same time; and in the event Sir Humphry Davy, the eminent scientist, and George Stephenson, the self-taught mechanic, simul-taneously produced lamps which were safe. Davy's was the result of scientific analysis of the problem, Stephenson's of practical experiments lasting only a few weeks, based on imperfect under-standing of the theory of the matter; but both worked, and each pattern was used for many years in coal-mines. Basically, the solution consisted in admitting the air to the burner only through some perforated material—usually metal gauze in Davy's lamp, a cover drilled with holes in Stephenson's. Neither allowed the flame to pass outwards and ignite the gas which might be present. The immense value of the invention was understood at once; in 1816 a public testimonial of £2,000 was presented to Davy, with 100 guineas as a kind of consolation prize for Stephenson. This aroused such feelings on Tyneside that a subscription was got up for Stephenson, which raised £1,000. He was obliged to accept the presentation at a public dinner and make a speech, a thing which seemed to him a frightening ordeal. 'You could have lit a candle at my face,' he said of the occasion. (In later years he lost his reticence and delighted to talk in public of his early struggles.) The occasion brought out the Grand Allies and other notable people of the North-East to do him honour; and George Stephenson's name and reputation began to be known outside the small circle of colliery managers on Tyneside.

3
Stephenson and the locomotive

◆

George Stephenson is often remembered as 'the father of the loco-motive'; but in that simple form the statement is untrue. If any single person can be said to have invented the steam locomotive, Richard Trevithick, the Cornishman, must be given the credit; for on 21 February 1804 an engine designed and built by him hauled a train conveying 10 tons of iron over 9½ miles of tramway from Pen-y-darran, near Merthyr Tydfil in South Wales, to Abercynon wharf on the Glamorganshire canal. Writing about a trial trip a few days earlier, Trevithick said: 'It worked very well, and ran up hill and down with great ease, and was very manageable. We had plenty of steam and power.' These, however, were the words of a fond parent, not of an impartial reporter; there was a great deal more to be done before the locomotive was manageable, still more before it was economical. Trevithick had certainly shown that it was tech-nically possible to construct a steam engine that could move itself and a train of wagons along a prepared track, with a smooth wheel on the tram-plate type of rail. The inherent difficulty was that if the locomotive was heavy enough to secure adhesion – that is to say, to ensure that its driving wheels did not slip round when power was applied to them – then the track was too light to sustain the weight, and it broke. Until the track of the railway could be made firm and robust enough to support the locomotive, progress was going to be slow and ideas were going to be confused. George Stephenson had something very important to contribute in the way of improving the track and also a number of valuable features in regard to the mechanical design of the locomotive itself; but it was Richard Trevithick who first practically demonstrated three most important things: that a steam engine with smooth wheels could be made to travel and haul a load along a smooth railway track; that it could be driven with wheels on more than one axle coupled together; and that the steam, after it had done its work in driving the pistons in the cylinders, could be turned into the chimney in such a way that it helped to draw in air through the fire and so keep the fire lively.

These three features were of the greatest importance, and they have remained fundamentals of steam locomotive design; but the first twenty-five years of the history of the locomotive, from Pen-y-darran in 1804 to the famous *Rocket* of 1829, did not show straightforward progress. On the contrary, a number of lines of development that we can now see to have been blind alleys had to be tried and discarded, and progress was disappointingly slow, so that steam traction had not won the day by the end of the 1820s–indeed, it needed all the enthusiasm and skill of its advocates to persuade the directors of the Liverpool & Manchester Railway, due to be opened in 1830, to adopt locomotive traction; and it was a narrow thing, as we shall see.

Several reasons can be found to explain this apparent sluggishness in the development of the machine that Trevithick had taken so astonishingly far at his first serious attempt. The problem of the track on which the engines were to run was the most serious; wooden rails, sometimes covered with iron plating, precariously and unequally supported by 'dormant timbers' (or sleepers), were inadequate support for moving steam engines, especially when the engines had no springs to take care of irregularities in the road levels. Secondly, the demands of the designers had outrun the capacity of the little local workshops to produce the parts required; only the simplest boiler flues and cylinder castings could be reliably manufactured, and joints which would not allow steam to escape through them were almost impossible to make and maintain. The early locomotives were very poor performers at load-hauling; they clanked along at walking pace or less, making a great noise with their exhausts and with their cumbrous, inefficient gearing, and usually enveloped in clouds of steam escaping from places which should have been steam-tight. Much of this was due to inaccurate manufacture of parts and to consequent unwillingness of the engineers to trust more refined designs.

Then there was a good deal of personal jealousy between the different men at work on steam engines, and between different districts (echoed for many years later as controversy went on about precisely who invented this or that); though there was a great deal of discussion among the different Tyneside men at work on locomotives, and ideas were freely exchanged. Then, it may well be true that progress was comparatively slow because all those concerned were practical mechanics; it is possible that if a trained scientist had turned his mind to this subject (like Humphry Davy with the miner's lamp) he would have perceived which was the right road to follow much sooner than the trial-and-error man did. Against this, the record of trained scientists in respect of locomotives and railways when they had been perfected by the practical men does not give much encouragement to the idea that they would have done better. Dr Dionysius Lardner of University College, London, gave a good deal of attention to railways in the 1830s and generally contrived to make himself look silly (until he forsook the natural sciences for economics and then produced *Railway Economy*, which was really valuable). The early years of the internal combustion engine and the motor car show how, even after the principles which we now know to hold the key were discovered and applied, many other ideas seem attractive and have to be put to the test before they are discarded. The 'survival of the fittest' in engineering is a slow and rather wasteful process, but it seems that it has always to be gone through.

What exactly did George Stephenson contribute during those early years of the locomotive that proved to be of lasting value? His first and most famous biographer, Samuel Smiles, claimed for him the invention of the blast-pipe – the simple and (in its engineering meaning) elegant device by which the exhaust steam on its way to the chimney was made to draw air from outside in through the fire. As later locomotive engineers were to say, the first thing a steam engine must do is to boil water fast enough to maintain its output of power, and to be 'short of steam' is the worst fault of any loco-motive. But the blast-pipe was present in Trevithick's first engine, and he had recognized its importance; Stephenson cannot have the credit for that. If Stephenson did not re-invent the device (for there is some evidence that Trevithick visited Stephenson between 1805 and 1808, and can these two have failed to discuss the locomotive?), he may be allowed to have reapplied it to his *Blucher* engine in 1815; there it rather overdid its work, tending to pull the fire through the single boiler-flue and throw it up the chimney. After experience of *Blucher*'s working, Stephenson turned the exhaust steam from the two cylinders into the chimney through a pipe with a narrowed mouth. The modern blast-pipe, shaped and placed in such a way as to produce the greatest benefit in the classic form of locomotive boiler, was Timothy Hackworth's development in 1827.

What Stephenson did contribute in the years 1810–20 was still important enough. His chance came when a locomotive for the Killingworth wagon-way was ordered to be built in the West Moor colliery workshops. It was constructed under Stephenson's supervision and put to work on 25 July 1814, named *Blucher* in honour of one of the heroes of the day (there were already a *Lord Wellington* and a *Marquis Wellington* at work on the Middleton Railway, near Leeds, which had four steam locomotives by John Blenkinsop and Matthew Murray in 1812–13). As originally put to work, *Blucher*'s only striking novelty in comparison with locomotives of other builders at work at Wylam and elsewhere was that it had flanged wheels which rested on the top of 'edge' rails – that is, upraised rail surfaces of the modern type. Although this is the original form of railway, it had at the end of the eighteenth century been largely given up for the type with flat-tread wheels running on plate-rails of ⌐ and ⌐ shape, with the guiding flanges on the track itself. Except at Middleton, this method had been adopted for all locomotives so far.

Blucher's inadequate performance in its early state of development – the engine was certainly modified, perhaps more than once – probably turned Stephenson's mind to a number of improvements, some of detail and some important enough to be called matters of principle, which led to two patents he was concerned in. The first, in February 1815, jointly with Ralph Dodds, was for direct drive from the cylinders to the wheels through cross-heads, connecting-rods, and crank-pins (which almost at once became the usual method of drive for all steam engines), replacing the complicated and inefficient gears and chains of previous practice. The second, jointly with William Losh, chief proprietor of the Walker Ironworks, Newcastle, was for 'steam springs' – really cushions formed by the steam in the boiler. This line of development was not followed, but until laminated springs – that is, those built up with a number of leaves of high-quality metal laid on top of one another – could be satisfactorily produced, this invention had some value; it certainly showed that Stephenson knew that the absence of satisfactory springing was a serious weakness. This same patent also covered an improved form of wheel and an improved type of rail and supporting chair. In this last particular, Stephenson showed himself to be concerned not only with the locomotive as a machine but with the railway as a whole entity – an important pointer to the days not so far ahead when he would be engineer-in-chief for complete railway undertakings, covering both civil and mechanical engineering and also advising in many respects on what would later be called general management. It is also notable that responsibility for the *Blucher* and his work leading up to the two patents had not excluded other creative activity—the miner's safety-lamp experiments were going on between October 1815 and the end of the year.

At this point the career of George Stephenson seems to the historian to take a pause, and possibly a pause was perceptible to him. Smiles suggests that he thought again of emigrating to America with a view to building steamship engines there. Locomotive railways did not spread rapidly, in spite of the example of Killingworth; in fact, from 1815 to 1825 Stephenson seems to have been quite alone in struggling to improve and perfect the locomotive. It is for this reason, and not because of any radical invention, that J. G. H. Warren's statement is justified: 'George Stephenson more than anyone helped to establish the practical success of the locomotive and ensure its adoption in place of the fixed engine.' He claimed in 1825 to have built some fifty-five engines, of which 'about sixteen' were locomotives. Twelve are known for certain, all delivered to the North-East except one in 1816 for the Duke of Portland's Kilmarnock & Troon Railway—the first locomotive in Scotland. But no others were being built by anyone; the locomotive was a sickly child, and George Stephenson brought it through its infancy.

His reputation had at any rate spread outside the immediate Tyneside district, for he was appointed in 1819 as engineer to the Hetton Colliery Company, in County Durham, to design and equip a railway from the colliery to the River Wear, near Sunderland, some 8 miles, with a mixture of traction: 'self-acting' inclines, on which the weight of laden wagons running down was used to draw up empty wagons on the other end of the same rope; stationary engines hauling cables to which wagons were attached; and sections for locomotive haulage, on which five Stephenson engines were put to work in 1822–5. He laid down other short railways in the area, and was able to invest some capital in a colliery, a foundry, and land. He was drawing a number of different salaries and various fees, and his testimonial of £1,000 for the safety-lamp had provided him with a lump-sum of capital. He was able to send his son Robert, who on leaving school had been apprenticed to Nicholas Wood, the mining engineer who was 'head viewer' at the Killingworth collieries, to Edinburgh University for six months in 1822–3 to study natural sciences. Stephenson had arrived at a certain standing in the North-East; he was a person of importance in the somewhat limited engineering circle of the region; and he was ready for whatever opportunity might next come his way.

4

The Stockton & Darlington Railway

◆

The next opportunity was not long in coming. It was the Stockton & Darlington Railway, often referred to as the world's first public railway. It was not exactly that, for the Middleton colliery line at Leeds had been sanctioned by an Act of Parliament in 1758. That Act was, however, a means of overcoming legal difficulties about wayleaves; the earliest public railway in the modern sense was the Surrey Iron Railway, which had been accepting public traffic between Croydon and Wandsworth since 1803. Nevertheless, the Stockton & Darlington did mark an important step forward in the conception and the practice of railways.

The name – Stockton & Darlington – can be a little misleading. The railway did link the two towns, the former on the navigable Tees, the latter some 9 miles inland, in south Durham; but its purpose and justification lay farther on, at the coalfield lying around Bishop Auckland, in the valley of the Wear about 12 miles north-west of Darlington. The Wear Valley did not present a satisfactory route for Auckland coal – the river was never navigable above Durham – and Sunderland at its mouth was nearly twice as far away from Auckland as Stockton was. But between the Auckland pits and the Tees lay some highish ground, and various canal schemes which had been proposed from time to time since 1768 had never come to anything. From 1810 onwards Edward Pease, a Quaker banker of Darlington, took up a railway scheme to link the Auckland area with Stockton by way of Darlington – which lay away to the south of the direct line of route, though the diversion offered easier gradients. Anyway, if the Darlington Quakers' money was to go into the line, it must run by Darlington; and as their money was essential, that settled the route. When George Stephenson once suggested to Pease that the shortest line to the collieries would run somewhat farther north, the Quaker pulled him up firmly: 'George,' he said, 'thou must think of Darlington; thou must remember it was Darlington sent for thee.'

The promoters had a hard time from 1810 to 1820, first in finding

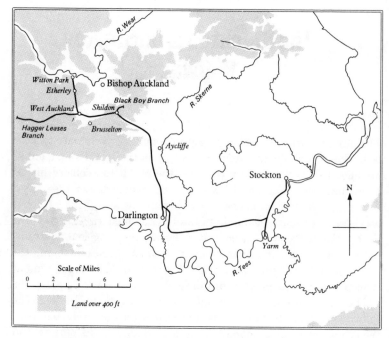

The Stockton & Darlington Railway's original lines

an engineer they could get on with, and then in marshalling their
supporters in and out of Parliament to secure the necessary Act to
enable them to acquire the land necessary for the line. (Railways
could be made without Acts of Parliament, on a single owner's
property, or when all the landowners on a given line agreed; but
without an Act, construction of a line of railway could be frustrated
if one landowner on the line of route declined to sell the necessary
land or grant a wayleave; with an Act, the railway could insist on
purchasing.) The first attempt to get an Act failed; the second, based
on plans drawn up by George Overton from far-away Breconshire in
South Wales (who had had much experience in laying down quite long
lines of plate-rail tramroads), was passed into law on 19 April 1821.

George Stephenson had nothing to do with the inception of this
project; but he must have known what was going forward, and
equally the promoters can hardly have failed to know about him.
His reputation must have spread through the county of Durham,
particularly since his contract for the Hetton Colliery line. On the

day that the Royal Assent was being given to the railway's Bill in London, he had an appointment to meet Edward Pease at his home at Darlington, and he took the precaution of walking the route from Stockton beforehand. Pease appears to have understood the engineer's quality at this first meeting. 'There was such an honest sensible look about George Stephenson,' he wrote, 'and he seemed so modest and unpretending, and he spoke in the strong Northumberland dialect.' (The language of Tyneside can still be rather difficult for other people to understand.) It seems that at this meeting Pease quickly decided that Stephenson would be a better man for the railway work than Overton, and that he would recommend him to the other directors for the appointment of superintending engineer – that is, to survey the line afresh, make plans and estimate the costs of the work, see to the letting of the different contracts, and

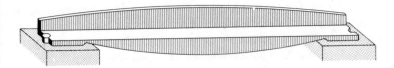

Cast Tram Rail, Surrey Iron Railway, 1803

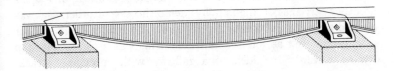

Losh and Stephenson's Patent Cast Rail, 1816

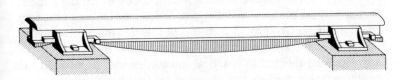

Stephenson's Wrought Iron Rail, Liverpool & Manchester Railway, 1829 (from C. E. Lee, *The Evolution of Railways*)

supervise their execution. During the interview, it appears also that Stephenson firmly stated his belief in the advantages of the railway—that is, the edge-rail rather than the plateway or tramroad—and urged Pease to consider traction by locomotive engine on the more level parts of the line. Stationary engines, winding wagons attached to cables up or down, were intended for crossing two ridges (Etherley and Brusselton) at the Auckland end, and these were installed and used for many years.

How far all these matters were explored at the first meeting between Pease and Stephenson is not known; but the impact of Stephenson's personality on the shrewd, honourable, and influential Quaker was decisive. Stephenson became the new railway's engineering adviser, and in time all that he recommended was adopted. Alterations were made in the proposed line of the railway, to avoid some gradients (this became a characteristic of all the Stephenson lines) and to provide an even closer approach to the town of Darlington. Edge-rails were adopted, mostly of wrought iron, not cast iron; this was a change that he had conscientiously to recommend, but it went against his own financial interests, for it turned his former associate William Losh into an opponent. Finally, the company decided to try locomotive engines. Edward Pease went over to Killingworth in the summer of 1822 to see locomotives at work; and what he saw convinced him that the experiment should be made on his line. This led to a significant clause in the amending Act of 1823, whereby the original reference to the hauling or drawing of wagons and other carriages on the line 'by men or horses, or otherwise' was enlarged to a specific permission to employ locomotive engines, for passenger as well as for freight traffic. This was a significant step forward towards the idea of a railway with specialized track, mechanical power, and accommodation for public traffic, which was the railway as later ages have known it; but, nevertheless, the Stockton & Darlington, when it was opened in 1825, was in some ways closer to the old conception of a toll-road on which the owners, who maintained the fixed installations, levied tolls for use of the way from the carriers who provided their own vehicles and motive power. The railway company provided some, but by no means all, of the motive power; this led to practical difficulties and disputes on the line in operation, and so demonstrated that all power on a railway must come under a single control.

While the Stockton & Darlington was under construction, George

Stephenson took two decisions that were critical for the future development of his own and his son's careers. For the thorough survey which he undertook in the autumn of 1821, George stipulated for adequate assistance. John Dixon was his first choice, Thomas Storey the second; and another was Robert, then aged eighteen and suffering somewhat from ill-health brought on by his work, often underground, as apprentice at Killingworth pit. His confidence in the young man was justified by the result, and in 1823 Robert (who had in the interval assisted on a survey for a railway from Liverpool to Manchester) signed as engineer on the plans of the Hagger Leases branch line and saw them through the Parliamentary committee. His charge to the company for this service was 15 guineas plus a guinea a day and expenses for attendance on thirty-four days while the Bill was in Parliament. His career as a civil engineer had begun.

The second decision was equally important for the future of railway engineering. George Stephenson was determined to keep the manufacture of steam locomotives alive and under his hand; but during these years no workshop was willing to tackle his locomotive work—he had parted company with Losh and his Walker Foundry over the matter of wrought-iron rails. He had entered into partnership with John and Isaac Burrell, Newcastle ironfounders, but this firm apparently built no locomotives. It was natural that he should try to interest his new Darlington friends in establishing a locomotive works of their own. He succeeded in persuading Edward Pease and Michael Longridge, of the Bedlington Ironworks, to become partners with himself and his son in a £4,000 venture, which in the event paid them all handsomely. More surprisingly, perhaps, the firm was called Robert Stephenson & Company, and twenty-year-old Robert became managing partner, at a salary of £200 a year, in full charge of the factory, with advice on design matters from his father. The Forth Street works in Newcastle began operations late in 1823 or early 1824 with orders for an 8-hp engine for a Mr Bragge (otherwise unknown), a 15-hp engine for 'the Stockton steam-boat', and two stationary engines for the Stockton & Darlington Railway, followed by two locomotives for the railway in 1824 and two more in 1826. From that time until 1963 the firm and its successors held a place in the front rank of private locomotive manufacturers in Britain. It was the firm, and not George or Robert personally, that gave its name to the 'Stephenson Link Motion' for locomotive valve-gear, invented by William Williams and William Howe in 1842.

It may seem strange that the Stockton & Darlington Railway should have contracted with a firm in which one of its directors and its principal engineer were personally interested, and there was criticism of this from Stephenson's opponents (for he had opponents, and some enemies) at the time; but there was really no other course that the directors could prudently take. They had found their man, and they had to trust his inventiveness and his probity.

The works for the main line of the railway were pushed on through the wet winter of 1824–5, and the first engine, *Locomotion No. 1*, was tried with satisfactory results at Newcastle on 11 September 1825. Stephenson called it 'the Improved Travelling Engine'. It did not show any striking mechanical advance on previous Stephenson machines except that its four wheels were coupled by solid rods on their outer sides, which since then has been adopted as standard steam locomotive practice instead of the inefficient chains and sprockets formerly employed. It was delivered to the line of railway at Aycliffe by road, and with a locally-built passenger coach named *Experiment* made a trial trip on the day before the official opening. All went well, and on 27 September 1825 the Stockton & Darlington Railway was officially opened for passenger and freight traffic. It was a general holiday in the district, and great crowds turned out to witness the ceremonial of the opening. With no more than minor delays (unlike some later railway opening ceremonies, which kept invited guests out all day and half the night), *Locomotion* performed her work well, covering part of the distance at 8 miles an hour, some at 4 miles an hour, with a load of 80 or 90 tons.

So the Stockton & Darlington Railway was there for all to see: 'the great theatre of practical operations on railways', one of its visitors called it. Its inception and business management were due primarily to Edward Pease; its technical features were due to George Stephenson practically alone. It was a queer sort of railway, with mixed horse and steam traction, on which the company owned some of the passenger vehicles, local coach proprietors others, and individuals owned all but 150 of the wagons for conveying the coal. But it was a working railway, and people from many other places went to look at it and think hard about its possibilities. It represented the end of the beginning phase for railways; the next developments would carry them forward into the modern age.

5

The young
Robert Stephenson

◆

Up to this point the career of Robert Stephenson had been remarkable–indeed, precocious–by reason of the intensity of his father's drive to equip him with theoretical as well as practical engineering knowledge, and to force him to accept heavy responsibility at an early age. His experience in surveying and in the management of the engine works was giving him the best possible training for the new age of railway building that was almost certainly ahead, so far as shrewd observers in the early 1820s were likely to foresee. Yet at this very moment, with the firm of Robert Stephenson & Company just getting into its stride and clearly requiring the best management it could get, Robert decided to cut loose from England altogether and sign a three-year agreement as engineer to the Colombian Mining Association. His responsibility would be to lead an expedition to set up mines and equipment at Santa Ana, on the Magdalena River in Colombia. A leading promoter of the Association (which had just changed its proposed field of operation from Mexico to Colombia) was Thomas Richardson, a Quaker friend and cousin of Edward Pease, who was a wealthy man–he put up £5,500 of the Stockton & Darlington capital and arranged a loan to the company at a difficult time. He had possibly contributed (through Pease) one-fifth of the original subscription to Robert Stephenson & Company. As an original partner in the firm of Overend, Gurney & Co, he was an influential City figure, and he could bring effective pressure to bear on Pease and his partners, however reluctant, to release their brilliant young manager.

The minerals to be obtained in Colombia were more exciting than coal–gold, silver, copper, and tin were hoped for. In the 1820s Cornwall was dominant in the world's copper production–more than two-thirds of all supplies were mined there. It shared with the Dutch East Indies the world's production of tin; and the techniques of mining these valuable metals had been raised to a high pitch in the county. Accordingly, in the spring of 1824 Robert toured Cornwall and turned his observant mind to methods of mining that he had not seen in the coal-pits of Tyneside. Generally he found little that was superior; but this tour, undertaken at the Colombian Association's expense, was an essential preliminary to his expedition.

The decision to go to South America has seemed so surprising that it has been suggested that there must have been a 'rift in the partnership': that Robert was riled by his father's domineering ways, and possibly resented his treatment of William James, the man he had worked for on the Liverpool & Manchester survey, so much that he felt he must get away from the stifling effect of his father's strong personality, and that a clean cut was the only course to take. This explanation can only be a guess; there is no evidence whatever that it is correct. Against the suggestion, the early biographers' statement that his health was the reason cannot quite be dismissed; the Colombian climate, at the height where he worked, was so much better than that of Newcastle that the change may well have saved his life. Then it has to be remembered that Central and South America at that time stirred the imagination of adventurous men – the El Dorado of earlier centuries, the inexhaustible gold- and silver-mines which the newly-learned techniques of English mining could speedily exploit; and both Stephensons were still primarily mining men, locomotion above the surface being an adjunct to the main business of getting the minerals. Then there might well be valuable orders for machinery and equipment to be obtained for the new firm; in fact, an inquiry from Richardson had been received in October 1823. George saw Robert off at Liverpool with every appearance of cordiality; if there had been a rift between father and son, George was not the man to conceal his feelings with politeness. It seems most probable that the young man determined to go for valuable experience, and his father and the other partners (Pease and Longridge), though they regretted the decision and tried to dissuade him, did not maintain their opposition once they saw that his mind was made up. At all events, when Robert returned home in 1827 he stepped straight back into the managership of the locomotive works and partnership in the new undertaking of George Stephenson & Son (of which more later). There may have been some adjustment of his relations with his father at this time, as happens between many men in their early twenties and their fathers; but a 'rift' seems much too strong a word to give to the process.*

---

* Since the first publication of this book in 1966, a letter dated 23

The Colombian interlude in Robert Stephenson's life lies right outside the course of his development along the road to becoming Britain's leading railway engineer; and yet it may have had an important influence on the formation of his personality by bringing out his power of dealing with men. Robert always attracted devotion from those who worked under him; their feeling for George was more often respect than liking. The power of leadership and the ability to inspire affection were Robert's great strengths as a manager and administrator, quite apart from his technical ability, and these qualities were first given a chance to be exercised high up on the Colombian plateau from 1825 to 1827, when he had to deal with local officials and–much more difficult–a boisterous set of miners from the other extremity of England, from the tin- and copper-mines of Cornwall. The slight young northerner had to assert his power of personality over rough men who were almost as foreign to him as the Colombians were, in the knowledge that the enterprise was not prospering as its promoters hoped.

On the way to the mining area, he examined the possibilities of a breakwater at the port of La Guaira and a railway from it to Caracas, the Venezuelan capital (then part of Great Colombia). He reported against both these projects. He arrived in Bogotà, the 8,600-ft high Colombian capital, in January 1825, collecting mineral samples on the way. His little party then went on by mule, past piles of rusting machinery sent out for the mines on the mistaken supposition that there would be roads to move it along to Mariquita and Santa Ana. Here, in a beautiful climate, he had a bungalow built of bamboo with palm-leaf roof, and here he made his home for more than two years. The Cornishmen learned to respect the young man, who showed that he had the moral courage to stand up to them and the physical strength to take part in their sports, and often beat them. But he could not stop them drinking to excess, and he never had more than two-thirds of his labour force of 160 fit to work–the others had drunk themselves incapable.

February 1827 written in his own hand from George at Liverpool to Robert in Colombia has come to light and been published. Professor Jack Simmons, discussing it, concludes that it is consistent with my interpretation given above: J. Simmons, 'A Holograph Letter from George Stephenson', *Journal of Transport History*, new series I (1971–2), 108–115.

It was exhausting, disappointing work, and the news from home which he received by infrequent posts was often discouraging; but he was determined to stick out his time, and he did so. When the London promoters pressed him to stay on for a longer term, he was firm in rejecting their inducements, and he set off for home in July 1827, travelling via Cartagena on the Caribbean coast, where he met Richard Trevithick, the 'Cornish Giant', now aged fifty-six and out of luck after eleven years in search of his personal El Dorado in Peru and Costa Rica. Young Stephenson was able to give the father of the steam locomotive £50 to buy a passage back to England.

Robert had thought of visiting the isthmus of Panama to see whether a proposed canal from the River Chagres to Panama City had any prospects of advantage—so wide did his mind range, even after three years of exile—but he could not manage it; instead, he took ship for New York. The vessel was wrecked, but all on board escaped with their lives, though they lost most of their baggage. Undeterred by this experience, he and four friends decided to walk from New York via Niagara Falls to Montreal—about 500 miles—in order to see the country. The little party enjoyed the hospitality of the country people, but Robert found Canada far behind the United States in its progress. Returned from Montreal to New York, the party sailed for Liverpool in November 1827; and on arrival Robert went straight to the house which George was occupying in the town. George, at forty-six, was in the midst of the hardest struggle of his career, the Liverpool & Manchester Railway, and it looked as though he was beginning to prevail; Robert, at twenty-four, was active, thoughtful, and confident. The two might do much together.

1 George Stephenson: statue by E. H. Baily in the Great Hall, Euston Station (now demolished), photographed in 1883; now at National Railway Museum, York

2 Robert Stephenson: cast from a bust by E. W. Wyon

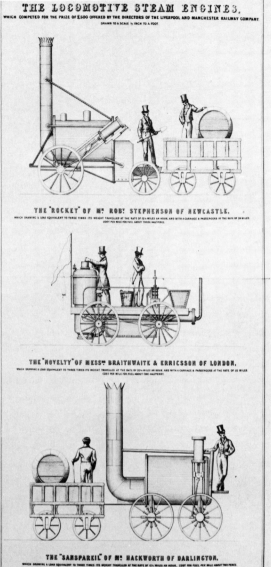

3 Broadsheet of the Rainhill Locomotive Trials (not contemporary, probably late nineteenth century)

Mechanics' Magazine,

MUSEUM, REGISTER, JOURNAL, AND GAZETTE.

No. 324.]   SATURDAY, OCTOBER 24, 1829.   [Price 3d.

"THE ROCKET," LOCOMOTIVE STEAM ENGINE OF
MR. ROBERT STEPHENSON.

4 The earliest known illustration of the *Rocket*, October 1829

5 An engine of the 'Planet' type, from Michael Longridge's *Remarks on . . . Iron Railways*, 1832

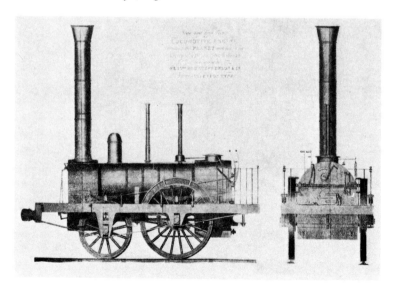

6 Working shaft in Kilsby Tunnel, London & Birmingham Railway, from a lithograph by J. C. Bourne, 1837

7 In the Olive Mount Cutting, Liverpool & Manchester Railway, from a lithograph by Crane

8 The opening day of the Liverpool & Manchester Railway, 15 September 1830, at Crown Street, Liverpool, from an etching by I. Shaw

9 The Britannia Bridge, Chester & Holyhead Railway, with Telford's Menai Bridge in the background, from an engraving by G. Hawkins

10 The High Level Bridge, Newcastle-on-Tyne, photographed about 1900

6
The Liverpool & Manchester Railway

◆

While Robert was away in South America, George Stephenson and his business friends, Edward Pease (acting apparently for Thomas Richardson as well) and Michael Longridge, made an agreement on the last day of 1824 to establish an office of engineering and railway surveying under the name of George Stephenson & Son. Robert was put down as an original partner, with the right to withdraw after his return to England if he wished. The original document stated that the two Stephensons should take charge of 'pointing out, and surveying, etc.' all lines of road (i.e. railroad), and there is nothing in it inconsistent with the position that George had taken up in regard to the Stockton & Darlington–that.the engineer appointed by the railway company should survey the line and prepare the plans and superintend their execution, but that the actual work of construction should be done by contractors. Later, especially on the Liverpool & Manchester line, this valuable distinction became blurred when George Stephenson himself, as the company's chief engineer, executed large parts of the works with labour directly employed by the company. It has been suggested that the crafty Quaker businessmen led the unsubtle engineer into this false position. It is possible, but there is no evidence. It is equally possible that his success in getting the job caused George Stephenson's head to swell somewhat, so that he became confident that he could not only superintend but also carry out the whole of the works himself.

The original intentions of George Stephenson & Son were ambitious enough. The first outline for the firm, written out by Michael Longridge (who was the business manager, being convinced that George and Robert were 'deficient' in habits of business), provided an establishment of nineteen named engineers and a secretary, apportioned to four proposed rail roads–'London and Northern', Liverpool & Manchester, Liverpool & Birmingham, and 'London and South Wales'. Only the second and third of these were live schemes, with applications made to Parliament; but the inclusion of the others was significant.

Proposals for railways of more than local interest were lively in the winter of 1824-5, when plenty of people were ready to invest money in schemes that normally would have been regarded as highly speculative. Hitherto, railways had been considered almost entirely as a means for moving heavy materials over short distances to navigable waterways; but now men like Thomas Gray of Newcastle, William James, and others were thinking—sometimes rather wildly—about much more exciting possibilities, even of a general, country-wide system of railway communication. The boom of 1825 broke at the end of the year, and the Liverpool & Manchester was the only one of the big schemes to survive; but Stephenson had already carried out surveys with his associates of lines between Leeds and Selby, Bolton and Leigh in Lancashire (the first public railway in Lancashire, opened in 1828), Canterbury and Whitstable in Kent (opened in May 1830), the narrow-gauge Nantlle Railway (a little mineral line in Caernarvonshire), and an extension of the Stockton & Darlington to Middlesbrough. As we recount the story of the Liverpool & Manchester, the Stephensons' next and in many ways their most significant work, it has to be remembered that they had these other commitments, as well as the running of the engine factory, always on their minds at the same time. In a written account their different works have to be considered separately; but life is not, in fact, so tidy. The Stephensons had to be constantly on the move, surveying land, superintending work, meeting individuals and committees, developing the steam locomotive and persuading doubtful people to give it a trial, and taking decisions from hour to hour about many different matters, unrelated to each other. This is what all managers have to do, in some degree; in their case, it must have needed almost superhuman powers of physical strength and mental concentration to carry them through with so few serious errors of judgement.

A characteristic letter of this period was written to the committee of the Bolton & Leigh Railway during its planning:

Liverpool Nov. 14th, 1824

Gentlemen,

Having duly considered the various Lines of the intended Road proposed to Mr. Steel and having the Sections of two before me the practicability of the one and the impracticability of the other is so

obvious that it is unnecessary to make any comment on either. The
red line represents the intended line of Railway on both Sections. I
am sorry I could not attend the meeting but I hope Mr. Steel will be
able to make any explanation that may be wanted. I am very confident
that the line I have laid out is the best that can be got.

I am Gentlemen
Your obt Sert
Geo: Stephenson

He was confident that he (or his assistant) had found the best
solution, and he expected the promoters to take his word for it.
Those who did so were rarely let down.

South Lancashire in the early 1820s displayed, in a particularly
acute form, an affliction that was beginning to exist in several parts
of Britain: transport starvation. The population of Liverpool
doubled between 1800 and 1825; that of Manchester and Salford,
some 33 miles inland, was rising still faster. Liverpool's seaborne
trade was growing fast, and the Manchester district's production of
cotton, with new steam-driven machinery, was soaring. But communication between the producing centre of Manchester and its
natural outlet to distant markets, Liverpool, was wretched. Although
1,000 tons of goods were reckoned to be moving every day between
the two places, freight transport by road was slow and expensive;
by canal it was, although cheaper, still very costly, and subject to
serious delays. There was, in modern terms, not enough transport
capacity to match the traffic offering. Schemes for horse-drawn
tramroads were already being propounded before 1800, but the first
effective steps towards a railway came in 1822, when Joseph Sandars,
a Liverpool merchant who was the driving force behind the line in
its earlier years (as Edward Pease had been to the Stockton &
Darlington), engaged William James to make a survey–on which,
as we have seen, he took Robert Stephenson as an assistant. James,
for whom Robert always kept an affection, was a far-sighted man
who too often overlooked the immediate obstacles in his path; and
though his gift for prophecy was impressive, his performance, and
the 'embarrassed' state of his own business affairs, determined the
Liverpool promoters to turn to George Stephenson as their engineering adviser. It was ironical for James that he had probably been the
man to make Stephenson's name known in Lancashire.

James's survey had been conducted in the face of difficulties that
the Stephensons had not met in Durham. There they had serious

conflict only with two landed proprietors; but the Lancashire project was opposed not only by landlords but also by the powerful canal interests whose future prosperity was clearly threatened. In addition, Manchester always remained lukewarm about the railway. James failed to get his survey completed in time for presentation to Parliament in 1822; but although the project lapsed in public, the promoters did not flag. They went to investigate railway practice and results in the North-East, and in May 1824 they engaged George Stephenson, issuing a prospectus in October and going to Parliament in the 1824–5 session. George saw that his commission for the Liverpool & Manchester was the biggest thing that he had ever been presented with, and he moved from Newcastle to a house in Upper Parliament Street, Liverpool, in June 1824.

A very rapid survey had to be made, and much of the detailed work was left to unskilled assistants. Serious deficiencies were revealed when the Bill and the plans came up for detailed examination by some of the best legal brains of the day, brought in by the canals and landowners to oppose the railway in the proceedings before the Parliamentary committee. George Stephenson was heavily cross-examined on many details which he had to confess he could not vouch for but had accepted second-hand from others. The survey was shown to be inaccurate in several important particulars; this, together with the scorn thrown on George's perfectly reasonable statement that 12 miles an hour might safely be achieved by steam engines and on his determination to carry the line across the quaggy Chat Moss (or marsh), secured the rejection of the Bill and humiliation for the engineer. It was a test of his character, and he rose to it, for, whatever he may privately have thought, he did not admit to any loss of confidence in public. The successful opening of the Stockton & Darlington in September of the same year must have given him new heart. At Liverpool, the directors had decided that a fresh survey must be made by someone with more professional standing, though Stephenson continued to be supported as practical engineer by a majority. George and John Rennie were appointed for the survey, and most of the actual work was carried out by C. B. Vignoles. Their plans were approved by Parliament in 1826, and after some shifting about George Stephenson emerged as the company's engineer with sole responsibility to the directors for the execution of the works and the equipment of the railway.

The line of route finally determined lay partly to the south of

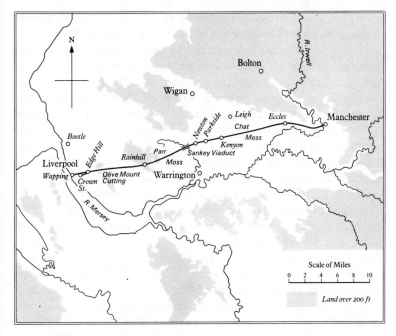

The Liverpool & Manchester Railway, 1830

Stephenson's route of 1824, but ran more directly from Crown Street, Liverpool, to the corner of Liverpool Road and Water Street, Manchester, 31 miles of double track in all. Abandonment of the northerly route, which would have provided a comparatively level and easy entrance to Liverpool via Bootle, meant that high ground immediately east of the town, at Edge Hill, had to be cut through. This called for a long tunnel (2,240 yards) from the waterside at Wapping up a gradient of 1 in 48 to Edge Hill. (This was worked in the early days by cable traction.) Passengers embarked at Crown Street, almost at the top. Great alterations have been made since the 1820s, and it is difficult to trace all these features today. But the impressive Olive Mount cutting, through the red sandstone about 1½–2 miles beyond Edge Hill, can still be seen from the train, though it has been widened to take four tracks. The Sankey viaduct was the most important bridge along the line, with nine 30-ft spans having a height of some 70 ft.

The great Chat Moss, and the smaller bog, Parr Moss, nearer

Liverpool, were to tax the patience and determination of George Stephenson and his backers to the utmost. The railway had in effect to be floated across the bog on a raft of brushwood and heather; but hundreds of tons of earth had to be tipped in before the raft was laid, and Stephenson refused to give up heart. His stubbornness beat the bog. The passage across the Moss and the tunnel at Liverpool were the first works to be started, in 1826. Early in 1827 the Olive Mount cutting and the Sankey viaduct were begun, and the expenses— which in the end amounted to about £820,000—rose alarmingly, beyond the capacity of the company to borrow money without backing. The directors succeeded in getting a loan from the Treasury to enable them to carry on—for in the early nineteenth century the State was prepared to lend money to assist in the building of certain types of approved public works, like canals, harbours, roads, railways, and the original Thames Tunnel. But the Treasury required their own engineer, Thomas Telford, who was the acknowledged head of the profession, to inspect the works and report on them. Telford in due course made an inspection, travelling over 30 miles of muddy and unfinished works on one January day in 1829, and found nothing to criticize as regards the civil engineering design and execution. But he found the management methods unsatisfactory— Stephenson was not applying the same excellent principles that he had insisted on for the Stockton & Darlington line; here, the company's engineer-in-chief was also a contractor. Most important, Telford was surprised to learn that it was still undecided how the line was to be worked when completed.

Indeed, it was high time for the directors to settle this vital point. George Stephenson had throughout urged the use of locomotive engines, but there was a determined group among the directors supporting fixed engines with rope haulage. Visits by deputations to the North-East did not produce any agreement, nor did the arrival and satisfactory working of Stephenson's *Lancashire Witch* locomotive on the nearby Bolton & Leigh Railway; so the Liverpool & Manchester board decided in April 1829 to offer a premium of £500 for 'the most improved Locomotive Engine'. Tests were conducted on a trial track at Rainhill, on the line of the railway, in October of the same year. The principal conditions of the trial were that a 6-ton locomotive must show itself capable of hauling 20 tons at 10 miles an hour for a sustained period; lighter engines smaller loads in proportion. A Stephenson engine, the *Rocket*, won convincingly. It was, in fact, the only one of the entrants to fulfil the conditions and to complete its trials without breakdown; in workmanship, if not necessarily in all points of design, it was markedly the best. Ten thousand spectators turned out to watch the fun and back their fancies. The Stephensons were not good showmen, and their engine was not the popular favourite; but Robert's time at Newcastle had been well spent. The earlier form of boiler had one flue, either single from back to front of the water-space, or with one U-shaped bend to return it again to the firebox end. With this arrangement, the hot surface of the flue with which the water came into contact–the 'evaporative surface'–was limited, and the steam-raising capacity was low. But the *Rocket*'s boiler had twenty-five separate tubes, which called for a high quality of workmanship in manufacture. With this boiler, moreover, the engine could raise enough steam to run laps totalling 60 miles at 14 miles an hour with a load behind the engine of 12¾ tons (three times its own weight). On the last lap it had enough left in reserve, and its driver had enough confidence, to startle the judges and the crowd with a speed of 29 miles an hour. It was another case of simultaneous invention that Marc Séguin, the great French engineer, was producing a locomotive on the same boiler principle during the same months of 1829 for the St Etienne & Lyon Railway; but the *Rocket* was running her trials a week or two before Séguin's engine. The idea was apparently due to Henry Booth, not a professional engineer but the secretary of the Liverpool & Manchester Railway, and it had been attempted on some light steam engines for use on roads; but it was Robert Stephenson who overcame the manufacturing difficulties and first produced a satisfactory multitubular boiler for a locomotive.

The Rainhill trials of 1829 conclusively settled the motive power issue for the Liverpool & Manchester Railway, and for most railways in the world for many years ahead. George's persistence and toughness, allied to Robert's mechanical gifts, both as a designer and in the workshop, had set railways and locomotives on the lines they were to travel for a century and more; and when the firm supplied the *Planet*, with cylinders inside the frames driving on a cranked axle, to the railway late in 1830, all the primary features in design which were to stamp Britain's locomotives throughout the steam age were to be seen in one machine.

After the locomotive drama at Rainhill, the completion and opening of the railway to traffic on 15 September 1830 may now seem something of an anticlimax; yet the occasion certainly did not seem so to the men concerned. New problems—of business management and of safety in operation of the railway—arose which had to be dealt with urgently: accommodation for passengers and goods, stations, working rules, commercial policies. In these the Stephensons were not so directly concerned. The operating arrangements on the opening day, when the Duke of Wellington was present, were rough and not very ready. There was nearly a riot at Manchester; the police were anxious about what might happen when the ultra-Tory Prime Minister, the 'Iron Duke', was within range of the near-revolutionary Manchester mob, which was in an ugly mood because of the late arrival of the inaugural train. (William Huskisson, a prominent Liverpool man and former cabinet minister, had been killed when he stepped from the Duke's train on to the adjacent running line.) It was a memorable day, for all its mischances, and many people recognized it to be so. A fully-equipped public railway, to move persons and goods exclusively by steam power, was in existence between two of the most important centres in the nation's economy. Without the two Stephensons, it would not have been there at that date or in that perfected form.

7
Years of success

◆

The Liverpool & Manchester triumph did not mean that the Stephensons could relax and take life more easily. On the contrary, they were determined to exploit their chances to the fullest possible extent. They stood pre-eminent as the one firm of proven ability as makers and equippers of railways, and they may have become a shade arrogant about it. George, at any rate, seems to have resented the rise to any kind of prominence of engineers who did not accept either his leadership or his general approach to railway construction; even more, he disliked any sign of independence among those who had been in his employment. Joseph Locke, who became one of the three great figures of the second wave of railway construction, with Robert Stephenson and I. K. Brunel, of the Great Western, fell out with the elder Stephenson early on, and, as some of his schemes were directly competitive with the older man's and were preferred, there was some bitterness. It would, of course, have been impossible for George Stephenson & Son to retain all, or indeed the greater part, of the railway business in their own hands, for the 1830s witnessed a second railway boom, culminating in 1836, when a multitude of engineers, some good and some less good, flocked into the business. The Stephensons' standing and the quality of their performance secured for them a handsome slice of the work that was going.

The first serious set-back to a proposal for which George Stephenson had been engaged as engineer was on the Leeds & Selby Railway, which he had surveyed in 1825; a different proposal by James Walker was preferred to his and adopted in 1829. In 1830 the Stephenson firm was appointed engineers for a Sheffield & Manchester Railway, which had support from both Manchester and Liverpool and was in some ways to be an extension of the Liverpool & Manchester over the Pennines. The scheme included some very heavy gradients worked by stationary engines and ropes, and a long tunnel. After much argument it was dropped in 1833, and another proposal, engineered by C. B. Vignoles, was taken up instead.

The firm was more successful farther south, in Leicestershire, where a railway was under discussion which would link the coalfield near Ashby-de-la-Zouch with the town of Leicester. The promoters visited the Liverpool & Manchester and in 1829 appointed Robert (on George's suggestion) as their engineer. This railway, the Leicester & Swannington, was opened in 1832; it was the earliest portion of the amalgamation later known as the Midland Railway to be built as a public locomotive railway. George Stephenson's first inspection of the route had convinced him that it was a good proposition; he invested £2,500 in its shares and undertook to get more taken up in Liverpool (as the principal shareholder he later became a director), and he invested money in coal-pits at Snibston, close to the line near Coalville. This was one of his most successful investments and paid him handsomely. He left Liverpool in 1830 and moved to Alton Grange, a largish farmhouse near Coalville, so as to be close to his colliery properties. Here he lived during the 1830s, in a central position from which he could direct and visit all the scattered works under his control.

The three years 1834–7 were thought by his earliest biographer, Samuel Smiles, to have been the busiest in George's life. Though he spent six months of that time in London, he yet travelled over 20,000 miles by road, surveying possible new lines, supervising those in progress to his designs, and visiting the locomotive works at Newcastle. It would be tedious to list all the railways he surveyed or constructed, and no complete authoritative list is available. Even a mention of the principal ones that he engineered gives an idea of the man's formidable energy: the North Midland, from Derby to Leeds; the York & North Midland, from Normanton to York; the Sheffield & Rotherham; the Birmingham & Derby Junction; the Manchester & Leeds; the northern half of the Grand Junction, running southwards from the Liverpool & Manchester through Warrington towards Birmingham (Joseph Locke, his former pupil, to George's disgust getting the southern half). During this period he surveyed railways in north Wales, round the shores of Morecambe Bay in north Lancashire, in the south of Scotland, and from Basingstoke through Salisbury to Taunton. In 1836 no less than 214 miles of new railway were authorized to be built under his direction, involving expenditure of over £5 million. In 1839–40 these and other lines designed by him, amounting in all to 321 miles, were opened for traffic. Of course, he had assistants and a well-organized office; nevertheless, a personal responsibility lay on him for all this work, and any serious failure would have been fatal to his reputation. Here is a typical letter of this period, plain, direct, and brief;

Dear Gooch,

I remained too long in Wales to get back to Manchester before coming here. I have examined the Lines set out by Rastrick & Vignoles and recommended by the Irish Railway Commissioners, from Wolverhampton to Porton Clun [Porth Dinllaen] on the West Coast of Wales as the thoroughfare to Ireland, and I find it quite an impracticable scheme and intend giving them a severe rap about it—The difficulties which have been met with on the London & Birmingham Railway are trifles when compared with the Welsh Line. Tunnell, two Miles long thro an impracticable material namely Basaltic.

I have just received a letter from Naysmith & Co. a copy of my answer I enclose you.

Yours truly,
Geo: Stephenson

Newcastle Decr 14 1838

The output during this most productive period was massive. Can we discover any distinctive principles running through it? The most striking feature common to all the Stephenson proposals was a vein of hard common sense. This was a specially useful virtue during the 1830s, when ideas about railways were sometimes very wild indeed (including a number of notions for driving trains by sails, or other applications of wind power); but Stephenson had learnt railways the hard way, and he knew what he knew. Bright ideas did not impress him much unless he could see how they fitted into his scheme of things; that is, they must be developments of his kind of railway, not divergences from it. What was more, he was concerned to see that the railway when built would pay; he was not the kind of engineer who would take his money for construction if he thought that the investment was going to turn out a bad one for the owners.

He was convinced that the original gauge of the north-east coast must be adopted as standard throughout the country. (The Stockton & Darlington's 4 ft 8 in between the rails got eased out by another half-inch at some point which is not quite certain. Vehicles built for the earlier gauge would, of course, ride quite easily, because of the width of the tread of the wheel-rims, on a slightly wider rail spacing.) Lines were built by different people to 4 ft 6 in Scotland, with one example (the Fordell Railway) of 4 ft 4 in, 5 ft in East Anglia, and even 7 ft (plus a quarter-inch) in the West of England; but Stephen-

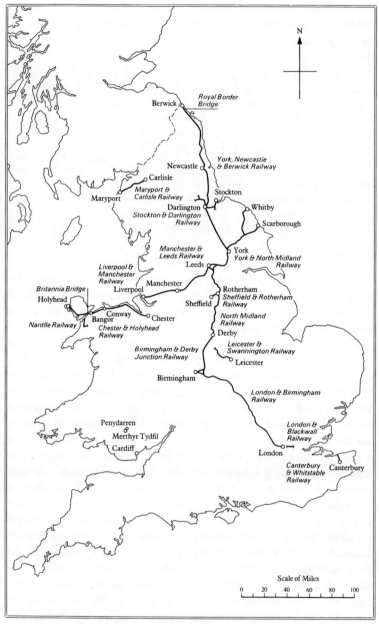

The principal Stephenson railways in England and Wales

son lines had to be standard gauge, for all the railways, he was convinced, would meet one day and traffic would be exchanged over them throughout Britain. This is exactly what happened within a very few years.

Then, Stephenson avoided heavy gradients for main lines. He would always go round rather than over an obstacle if he could. The locomotives of his day were inefficient enough to make this a reasonable precaution, though other engineers did not abhor gradients so much as he did; but he always disliked the wastefulness inherent in using two engines to drag a train up a hill when one would be enough on a flatter, if longer, route. This propensity led him to adopt a route for the North Midland Railway, linking Derby and Leeds, that missed Sheffield altogether and left it to be served by a connecting line from Rotherham, 6 miles away to the northeast. His Morecambe Bay scheme, the unsuccessful rival of Locke's route from Lancaster to Carlisle over the difficult grades by Shap summit, would have kept on the level all the way round the west Cumberland coast. He linked his scheme for an embankment across Morecambe Bay with a project for drainage and cultivation of the land thus reclaimed which was imaginative and might still be carried out with advantage today.

On the other hand, he was not hidebound about motive power. He believed in steam haulage for main lines; but for lines of purely local importance, or with a special character of their own, common sense told him that other forms of traction still had their uses. The Whitby & Pickering Railway, trundling across the north Yorkshire moors, was designed by him for horse-traction in 1832; what traffic was likely to arise needing anything more forceful? (He was investing in this district also—he had an interest in the Whitby Stone Company.) He was quite content to adopt stationary-engine and rope working for steep inclines on mineral railways; and he appears to have recommended this form of motive power for his only suburban railway, the London & Blackwall, opened in 1840. As it was to be completely self-contained, with short-distance passenger traffic only and no goods traffic, he apparently accepted that a 5 ft gauge would do it no harm. He was even prepared to accept electricity for railway traction; if a report of a conversation is true, he said 'electricity would be the great motive power of the world'. But as for the 'atmospheric' railway, using air propulsion, which Brunel was advocating, he just said: 'It won't do.'

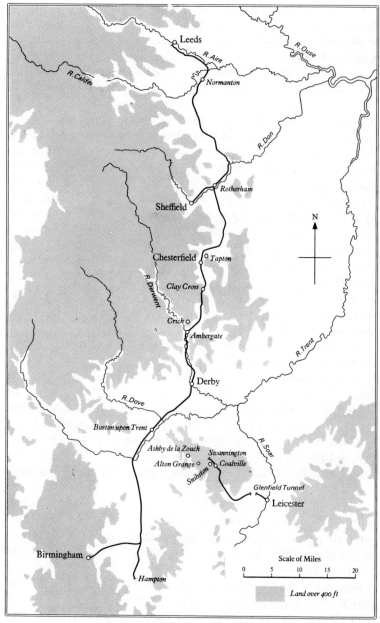

Stephenson railways in the North Midlands

George Stephenson first met the railway promoter and speculator George Hudson in the year 1834. Hudson, a 'self-made man' who started his business career as a linen-draper in York, did as much as any man to shape the main physical outlines of the English railway system in his heyday before his financial collapse and disgrace in 1849. Stephenson, who was never himself a promoter but always executant of other men's projects, was associated with Hudson in all the Midland Railway schemes and in the difficult and delicate business of linking up different lines, existing and not yet built, to produce the East Coast Route of railways to Scotland, through York, Newcastle, and Berwick to Edinburgh. What did these two think of each other?

Certainly Hudson valued Stephenson's judgement; even more he valued the advantage that his name and standing gave as support to the schemes he was promoting. Stephenson seems to have liked Hudson well enough, and he may well have been impressed with the man's vision of amalgamated, unified railways which he foresaw must eventually take the place of the locally-run small concerns that were typical of the 1830s. By about 1845, however, when Hudson controlled over a quarter of all the railways open in England, the older man must have felt as though his career could not last at the pace—not all the lines in the Hudson empire were soundly based on good finance—and his friendship turned to distrust before the end. But before that happened, the two men had been very useful to each other.

One result of Stephenson's connexion with the North Midland Railway (which became a Hudson line, though Hudson did not launch it) was that he moved from Alton Grange to Tapton House, Chesterfield, early in 1843. His lifelong knowledge of minerals and mining had endowed him with a keen nose for a good investment in this field, and with George Hudson, Joseph Sandars of Liverpool, and William Claxton as partners he invested in coal-mines and iron-works at Clay Cross, limestone at Crich, and lime-works at Amber-gate, all near Chesterfield. These activities flourished, and they engaged most of the attention that Stephenson gave to business in his last five years.

Here in the time that was left to him George Stephenson lived in virtual retirement from railway affairs, apart from visits abroad. He went twice to Belgium in 1845, and made a long tour through the north of Spain later the same year—a difficult journey which shook his health – and another, with Joseph Paxton, to Austria in 1846. He took, however, a principal part in the foundation of the Institution of Mechanical Engineers at Birmingham in 1847, and he was its first president. At Tapton he was visited by all kinds of people, friends of his boyhood, men of business, and young engineers. He indulged the Victorian rich man's passion for gardens, building hothouses to produce fruits that should rival Paxton's from the Duke of Devonshire's estate at Chatsworth, not far away. He was annoyed that he could not make cucumbers grow straight, but in the end he baffled the wayward vegetable by enclosing it while growing in a cylindrical glass tube. He exulted in his success – 'I think I have bothered them noo!' he said. His mind turned more to imaginative schemes in his closing years than at the height of his career; he engaged in experiments with manure and stock-breeding, artificial incubation of eggs, and quick fattening of chickens; and he also seems to have contemplated making gas from coal at the pithead and supplying it by trunk main to London.

He lived quietly, going away only for railway openings and dinners and for agricultural shows and meetings. He enjoyed simplicity, perhaps to the point of affectation, and he liked to disconcert people with blunt affirmations of his modest origin. He held to no very strong religious views – apparently the disputatiousness of ministers had disenchanted him. He said in reply to an appeal for foreign missions: 'I will send the locomotive as the great missionary over the world.' Edward Pease regretted a tendency to intemperance in the old man – but the Quaker, though he was not a total abstainer, probably adopted an exceedingly strict standard. His wife Elizabeth died in 1845, and in 1848 he was married for the third time – to Ellen Gregory, who had been his housekeeper. There is a hint that Robert did not care for her. George Stephenson died at Tapton on 12 August 1848, aged 67, and was buried in the chancel of Holy Trinity Church, Chesterfield, under a plain stone lettered only: 'G.S. 1848'.

8
London and Newcastle

◆

To complete the story of George Stephenson, we have run very much ahead of his son's career, which we left soon after the opening of the Liverpool & Manchester. The next three years were busy ones for Robert. He was heavily engaged in the Newcastle works; in 1831, with the agreement of the Newcastle partners, he took a partnership with Charles Tayleur in a locomotive factory at Newton, near Warrington, better situated than Newcastle for business in Lancashire, and some of the Newcastle orders were transferred to Newton. Meanwhile, he was engaged with the Leicestershire railway and mining affairs; and three days after the Liverpool & Manchester opening he became associated with the London & Birmingham Railway. This appointment led to a decisive stage in his career, when he was seen to have made out an independent position for himself and no longer to be simply his father's right-hand man.

The idea of linking London by rail with the swiftly-growing manufacturing town of Birmingham had been put forward in the early uprush of railway schemes in 1825. It was revived in 1830, with two proposals, one for a line through Coventry, the other through Oxford and Banbury. George's opinion was sought, and he came down in favour of the Coventry route. The Stephensons were appointed to make surveys and plans for Parliament on 18 September 1830. In practice, it was Robert who carried out the surveys and appeared for the company before the Parliamentary committees; and when at length, at the second attempt, the line was authorized, he was appointed engineer-in-chief for its construction. His salary was at first £1,500, later £2,000 a year, and he had to devote virtually his whole time to the work. He moved to London, to a house on Haverstock Hill, and though he remained a partner in Robert Stephenson & Company, he was never again directly active in the business, and he relinquished his interest in Tayleur's (which later became famous as the Vulcan Foundry).

The task that he had undertaken was large, complicated, and

technically tricky. Over 100 miles of double-track railway were to be built concurrently, involving long and difficult tunnels at Primrose Hill (near the London end), Watford, and Kilsby (near Rugby), several viaducts and awkward bridges over canals and roads, great cuttings (as at Tring and Roade, the latter sometimes called Blisworth), embankments, station buildings, engine-houses, and water supplies, and finally, stationary engines and cables for hauling trains up the steep gradient from Euston to Camden Town. The undertaking was vastly greater in scale and scope than the Liverpool & Manchester–it represented when opened an outlay of £5½ million against £900,000 for the earlier line. It was, in relation to prices at the time, a bigger work than the MI motorway, which now runs close to it for a few miles; and there was no machinery to move the earth in the 1830s–everything had to be done by brawn and muscle.

The Primrose Hill tunnel, through the clay ridge of Hampstead, was the first difficult work. By using the best and most expensive

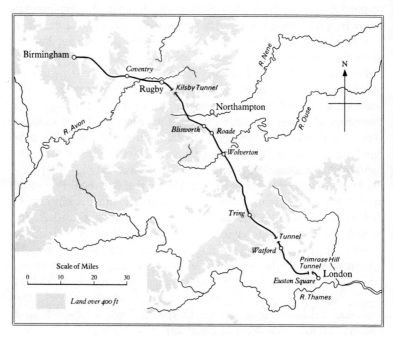

The London & Birmingham Railway, 1838

bricks, with cement instead of mortar, the tunnel lining was made strong enough to withstand the crushing force of the clay mass; but the cost was £280,000 against an estimate of £160,000. The cutting at Blisworth turned out to require 25 per cent more excavation than had been estimated; the Ouse Valley embankment at Wolverton slipped for months until it was stabilized, and then caught fire – alum shale, containing combustible material, was in it. The Grand Junction Canal held up railway operations by all means in its power, including recourse to law. The Kilsby tunnel, south of Rugby, 2,400 yards long, cost £320,000 against £99,000 estimated. On average, 12,000 men were engaged throughout the whole time on the works.

In the management of those under him on the London & Birmingham, Robert Stephenson's special gifts as an organizer of complex works first appeared. His practice of preparing drawings in great detail, drawn by his staff and issued to the contractors, was novel in its degree of precision, and it became standard on all important engineering works. His assistants, many of whom became well known in later years on their own account, were well organized, and quickly responded to the calls of their chief, who gave an example of strenuous activity, cautious judgement, and patience in personal dealings. The assistant engineers for the five districts into which the line was divided were John Birkinshaw, G. W. Buck, John Crossley, Frank Forster, and T. L. Gooch. These men and their young assistants called themselves 'Stephensonites', a band of brothers, who stood together and supported their leader in later controversies and triumphs. George could never have called forth the devotion these young men had for their chief. Devotion and loyalty were wanted, especially when things went wrong with the work.

A portrait of Robert Stephenson at this period, not by a 'Stephensonite' or a close associate, gives a cooler but probably juster description than those of his enthusiastic followers. F. R. Conder, then a very young engineer (he was twelve years junior to Robert), wrote:

'The personal appearance of that fortunate engineer is not unfamiliar to many of those whose eyes never rested on his energetic countenance, frank bearing, and falcon-like glance. It is rarely that a civilian has so free and almost martial an address; it is still more rare for such features to be seen in any man who had not inherited them from a line of gently-nurtured ancestors. In the earlier days of Robert Stephenson, he charmed all who came in contact with him. Kind and considerate to his subordinates, he was not without occasional outbursts of fierce northern passion, nor always superior to prejudice. He knew how to attach people to him: he knew also how to be a firm and persistent hater. During the whole construction of the London & Birmingham line, his anxiety was so great as to lead him to frequent recourse to the fatal aid of calomel.* At the same time the sacrifice of his own rest, and indeed of necessary care of his health, was such as would have soon destroyed a less originally fine constitution. He had been known to start on the outside of the mail, from London for Birmingham, without a great coat, and that on a cold night; and there can be little doubt that his early and lamented death was hastened by this ill-considered devotion to the service of his employers, and the establishment of his own fame. . . . He showed at times something of his father's determined and autocratic temper. He met his people with a frank and winning smile; his questioning was rapid, pointed and abrupt, and his eyes seemed to look through you, as you replied. Very jealous of anything like opposition or self-assertion, very unjust at times in suspecting such a disposition, he was disarmed by submission, and quieted by very plain speaking.'

These are the words of an admirer but not a worshipper; and they ring true.

At last, at high cost, the work was done, and in the autumn of 1838 the first main railway line from London was opened for traffic throughout. The Grand Junction Railway, continuing it north from Birmingham, was already at work, so that London was linked by rail with Lancashire. At the age of thirty-four, Robert Stephenson's name was made; men crowded to travel on the great new line of communication, and the London & Birmingham, which retained him as consulting engineer, set off on a prosperous career. But it had to pay for the suspicions of some of its directors about their engineer's interest in the locomotive works; the London & Birmingham ordered no engines from Stephenson's until 1845, and until then it relied on puny little machines built by Edward Bury, of Liverpool. The locomotive department was the weakest part of the concern; Stephenson was ostentatiously kept away from it.

If the London & Birmingham was on the way to prosperity, the engineer's own affairs were far from happy; indeed, at this time of professional triumph he must have had dark thoughts about his personal future. A singular misfortune had loaded him unsuspecting with a terrible embarrassment. This was an affair in County Durham,

---

* Originally introduced from the east, this drug was prescribed by English doctors at the time to cure practically everything; but it was probably useless rather than fatal.

not far south of Newcastle, called the Stanhope & Tyne Railway, which in its technical aspects was very much like previous railways built to carry coal from inland mines to the waterside: it was a colliery tramway, with some rope-worked inclines and some comparatively level sections to be worked by horses and by locomotives. Robert Stephenson agreed in 1832 to act as consulting engineer, and he accepted payment not in cash but in five £100 shares. Now the Stanhope & Tyne did not go to Parliament in what had become the normal way for incorporation on specified terms, as other railways were doing, but was a simple partnership acquiring by agreement 'way-leaves' for the line from landowners along the line of route. This meant, though Stephenson did not know it at the time, that if the concern got into financial trouble, each shareholder was liable for its debts up to an unlimited amount. By 1838 he realized that he was one of the few people connected with the line who was solvent; and at the end of 1841 he had to find £20,000 as his contribution to steadying its affairs, with no certainty that this would be the end of the story. When he should have been at the height of his success, the whole scene was clouded for him by this private financial embroilment. At the same time, too, he knew that his delicate wife, Fanny Sanderson (whom he had married in 1829), was desperately ill; she died in 1842, and he never married again. He left the Haverstock Hill house, first for Cambridge Square and then for No. 34 Gloucester Square, also in Bayswater, which remained his home for the rest of his life.

During the early 1840s Robert Stephenson was increasingly consulted about railways overseas, and he began to travel a good deal, building up friendships in France and helping to get more Stephenson locomotives purchased in many European countries–Austria, Belgium, France, Germany, Italy, and Russia already had some by 1840. In 1843 no fewer than eighty-one out of 180 English-built engines running in Germany had come from Stephenson's. His principal works at home in these years lay in the North-East, culminating in the building of the last link in the line of rails from London to the Tyne. The whole way from Euston Square through Rugby and following the Birmingham & Derby Junction route to York, Darlington, and Gateshead had been, either completely or in some measure, engineered by one or both of the Stephensons. On 18 June 1844 the Stephensons were given a rousing triumph on their own Tyneside. The Newcastle & Darlington Junction Railway was formally opened; flags were flown, cannon fired, church bells rung, and a great banquet followed the arrival of two trains, one with Hudson and his friends from York, the other through from London with the same day's newspapers in 8 hours 11 minutes (37 miles an hour throughout – a special effort, not repeated for some time). The speeches made at the dinner did full justice to the Stephensons and their part in perfecting the railway: rather more than justice, indeed, for the principal speaker credited George with the first railway locomotive. Local patriotism was prepared to forget Trevithick.

But the terminus of the junction railway lay at Gateshead, across the River Tyne from Newcastle. The railway age was forcing engineers to deal with tasks of bridging water gaps on a scale that had hitherto hardly been conceived; and bridging was to fill a large part of the next, and greatest, phase of Robert Stephenson's career.

9
The Great Bridges

♦

From 1844 to 1850 Robert Stephenson was incessantly, and simultaneously, engaged in the design of great railway engineering works, in public activity, and in the spread of his own business interests. For clarity, some account must be given of these matters separately; but it has to be remembered that they were all going on at the same time, pressing him to the utmost limits of his time and endurance. Yet, throughout, his nerve and judgement held.

Two matters of the first importance for the future development of the railway system were under acrimonious debate at the beginning of 1844: the question of gauge; and 'atmospheric' traction. There were Parliamentary inquiries into both these technical matters, for it was plain that diversity of practice between different railways would have important consequences which might be seriously against the national interest. The great champion of unorthodoxy in each case was I. K. Brunel. He was impatient of the limitations imposed by a gauge which was designed for working in and about coal-mines and convinced that the broad (7-ft) gauge had advantages more than offsetting the drawback of having more than one gauge in the country; and he was excited by the prospect of dispensing with locomotives in favour of propulsion by air-pressure, the train being connected to a piston running in a large pipe laid between the rails. Against him, on the side of accepted practice, in both cases stood Robert Stephenson. Brunel had a kind of intuitive engineering genius, leaping over objections based on experience and practice to novel and startling conceptions; Stephenson had no genius of that sort, but his immense talent for taking pains (which is a kind of genius) prevailed at the time and now seems to be of a harder-wearing quality. The two men were friends and supported each other at moments of personal crisis; but as engineers they stood, almost invariably, on opposite sides.

Stephenson's evidence on gauge was pithy and clear. He had once thought simply as an engine builder that, say, 5 ft would have been better than 4 ft 8½ in, but improvements since then had made that increase unnecessary; 4 ft 8½ in was fully adequate for any purpose to which a railway could be applied. Wherever a meeting of gauges took place, it must create a very serious inconvenience. This line of argument convinced the Commissioners, who reported accordingly (with a string of qualifications which left the Great Western free to go on extending the broad gauge within its territory, so that it lasted between Paddington and Penzance until 1892). At a series of trials with broad- and narrow-gauge engines that followed, the broad-gauge party had rather the better of things; but that could not alter Parliament's acceptance of Stephenson's view that uniformity of gauge in a country-wide railway system was worth everything. Australians, whose main railways were built on three different gauges because each colony chose its own, had no Stephensons to guide them; and the result is that the railway has not been able to serve Australia with all the expansive power that it would have exerted if it had been laid to one gauge throughout the continent.

On the 'atmospheric' railway – which was actually put into service in a few places: near Dublin, in south Devon, and between London and Croydon – Stephenson's verdict was brief and just: 'On long lines of railway the requisites of a large traffic cannot be attained by so inflexible a system as the atmospheric, in which the efficient operation of the whole depends so completely upon the perfect performance of each individual section of the machinery.' Brunel and other engineers were on the other side, and Stephenson did not convince all the promoters of new lines; he even had to resist a Brunel proposal for an atmospheric railway from Newcastle to Berwick, right in the heart of the 'Stephenson' country. That was defeated; the Croydon and Devon applications were failures; though the Dublin line worked well enough until 1854, it then became part of a through line worked in the normal way. The atmospheric idea was attractive, and able engineers supported it; but it depended for its success on a very high level of maintenance in mechanical condition, and this was a serious drawback. The orthodox Stephenson steam engine will work tolerably well, though not at full efficiency, when it receives a good deal less than first-class maintenance; and this was a great advantage in practical comparisons with rival systems, especially in the earlier period. Ruggedness, not delicacy, was its strength.

These two preoccupations were more or less out of the way by the end of 1846; but other kinds of public service were claiming Stephenson. In 1845 he became a commissioner for the industrial exhibition, finally held in Hyde Park with immense success in 1851, and he was on the building committee appointed in 1850. As soon as he was shown the original–indeed, startling–design for a great Crystal Palace produced by Joseph Paxton, the designer of garden hot-houses for the aristocratic plants of the Duke of Devonshire at Chatsworth, he supported it, and with this support it won the building competition. The first sketch for the design had been made on a piece of blotting-paper during a meeting of Midland Railway directors at Derby. In 1846 Stephenson reported on the possibility of building railways in Ireland as a measure to alleviate the misery and unemployment there in the famine year. He said that it should be possible to employ 90,000 men directly for four years in building a complete Irish railway system. Nothing was done at the time, though various British Governments down to 1914 continued to give financial support to railways in Ireland that, in ordinary economic terms, would have been better left unbuilt.

In 1847 Stephenson entered Parliament as a member for Whitby. He was a Tory of the Right–hostile to free trade, anxious to avoid change in almost any form. If this seems paradoxical in the man who was as much as any one person responsible for the great economic and social upheaval of his century, it must be explained by a tinge of scepticism, amounting to pessimism, which runs through all his later life. His approach to new problems was always cautious, and he had a genuine, not assumed, personal modesty; some people, while affecting to be modest, have a gift for 'backing into the limelight', but he did not do that. These characteristics are noteworthy in such a successful Victorian. He had little self-confidence (which shows that this quality is not essential in a great man), and he was inclined to undervalue his judgement and himself. He was a Tory because he was pessimistic and unsure of his judgement. He was for maintaining things as they were, not because he considered them good in their present state but because he felt sure that any change must be a blunder. Stephenson attended at the House of Commons fairly regularly, so far as his engagements would allow; he did not speak on specifically political issues but he contributed to debates when he thought his experience entitled him to be heard–on administration and organization, on railway matters, and on the Suez Canal.

As successful self-made men who had risen by the strength of their own efforts, it might have been thought that Robert and his father would have adhered to the pure *laissez faire* doctrine that the state should never intervene in business, especially railway, affairs; but, in fact, neither of them did so. George was by 1841 so much alarmed at unsafe methods of operation on the new railways that he advocated government control of signals (to impose uniformity), speeds, mechanical details, and in particular new inventions. Robert was driven by the inconsistency of legislation and its great expense to propose an expert board to deal with matters of railway policy. Competition, he flatly stated, had served no useful purpose. Neither George's scheme, in the form in which he put it forward, nor Robert's was adopted at the time, though later measures, brought in for other reasons, have led to very much the same result.

By 1850 Britain had well-developed railway communications linking all the important cities and industrial areas. Robert Stephenson's two last and greatest works at home were essential links in the chains from London to Edinburgh and to Holyhead (for the mail-boat passage to Dublin). By 1844 the rail had arrived at Gateshead, opposite Newcastle, and plans for the North British Railway from Edinburgh to Berwick were authorized in 1844 and for the Newcastle & Berwick in 1845. Robert was engineer to the latter, which included a splendid viaduct over the Tweed at Berwick, named the Royal Border Bridge when it was opened for traffic in 1850. (The border it spans is that between England and the town of Berwick-on-Tweed; the Scottish border is at Marshall Meadows, some 3 miles farther north.) This great bridge included no novelty in its design, for Stephenson experimented only when there was something tangible to be gained; but its twenty-six masonry arches make it, by its appearance of strength, regularity, and proportion, one of the most wholly satisfying, and at the same time romantic, of all railway structures.

The great bridge across the Tyne, built as a separate financial undertaking, had two levels of decking, one for railway and one for road traffic. The town centres of Newcastle and Gateshead are here separated by the River Tyne in its valley some 100 ft. deep, and the High Level bridge, as it was called, was designed by Robert with four spans over the river and one span with approach viaduct on each side. 'Bow-string' girders, with cast-iron arches (the 'bows') and wrought-iron straight members (the 'strings'), were used for the superstructure—a method already known and used elsewhere, but subjected in this case to the most exhaustive testing of the materials to be used. Little was then known about the strength of different constructional materials, and Stephenson had to devise tests of considerable ingenuity to determine how different kinds of iron would behave in this great structure; this meant 'testing to destruction', as it is called–finding what strain would break the material, and then deciding on a safe design in the light of that experience. He also introduced steam hammering for the foundations; this enabled a pile 33 ft long to be rammed home in the river-bed within four minutes and so considerably accelerated this part of the work. The bridge was opened for rail traffic in 1849 and stands today, carrying a volume of road traffic and weights of trains on the railway far beyond anything that its designer could have dreamed of. This is certainly creditable, but it is largely owing to multiplication of the 'safety factor' in the original design because of lack of precise knowledge of the materials being used.

By the time the great Tyne bridge was opened for traffic, the severest test of the engineer's nerve and competence had been in progress for some years. This was the bridge over the treacherous waters of the beautiful Menai Strait, the worst of the obstacles on the route of the Chester & Holyhead Railway, a line originally surveyed by George Stephenson in 1838. Robert Stephenson was associated with this undertaking from its incorporation in 1844 until its opening throughout in 1850. The Act of 1844 omitted any provision for crossing the Strait; it had been proposed to use Telford's elegant and slender suspension bridge for the mail-coach road, completed in 1826, for transference of railway carriages drawn by horses. This was clearly unsatisfactory, and Stephenson proposed a crossing about a mile from Telford's bridge, at a site where the Britannia Rock offered a footing in the middle of the stream. The Board of Admiralty, who jealously watched over shipping interests, insisted on a clear passage at least 100 ft high, not only at the centre of the spans but also throughout their length, so that any kind of arched bridge was out of the question. This huge clearance, which can hardly ever have been required, was related to tall sailing ships. It became clear that the span must itself be a girder (instead of a superstructure resting on girders), and by degrees the conception of a tubular beam–that is, a long hollow rectangular box through which the trains should run–was worked out. Stephenson felt confident enough about his conception to be able to convince a Parliamentary committee in 1845 that it was feasible; but he knew that more experimental and theoretical work on the properties of iron needed to be done, and he engaged William Fairbairn of Manchester, an engineer with much practical experience of iron construction, and Eaton Hodgkinson, later professor of mechanical engineering at University College, London, to conduct a detailed programme of testing. By early 1846 conclusions were emerging, and Stephenson put in hand the designs for a similar but much smaller bridge at Conway, which would serve in some ways as a rehearsal for the larger work. A scale model of the Menai bridge, one-sixth full size, was built and tested by hanging weights on it until the span collapsed. This occupied much of 1847, and working drawings for the tubes were made on the basis of the experiments with the model. Manufacture of the iron tubes, very large and at the same time precisely specified, was a task calling for new application of production skill; Charles Mare of Blackwall on the Thames produced all the tubes except one from Garforth of Manchester.

In the middle of all these preparations an accident happened which for a time shook Stephenson's normal composure. On 24 May 1847 an iron bridge designed by him for the Chester & Holyhead Railway just outside the city of Chester collapsed under a train. The design was defective, and Stephenson was virtually on trial at the inquest on the five people killed; the heavy strain on him was relieved only by the support of his brother engineers, Brunel, Locke, Vignoles, and others. He maintained that the bridge must have sustained some heavy blow, as if the engine's tender had been derailed by a wheel breaking. The jury's verdict was 'accidental death', and no open reproach lay on the designer; but he knew he had been at fault, and later implicitly acknowledged it.

As the Menai design was finally worked out, the water-crossing of about 1,000 ft was to be spanned by eight tubes in all, four for each line of railway. Three tower-like piers were built, one on each shore and one standing on the Britannia Rock at the halfway point. The principal tubes over the water were 460 ft long, those at the landward ends 230 ft. How to hoist them up into their final position was a problem requiring as much anxious thought as the design itself. The towers were originally designed to carry chains for use in the erection of the tubes; in the event, jacks and not chains were employed, but the additional height given to the towers above the tops of the tubes adds greatly to the architectural effect of the whole structure.

In preparation for the most dramatic of all the scenes in Robert

Stephenson's life, the floating into position of the great tubes for the water spans, a large model was made in 1848 so that the whole delicate operation could be studied in detail. The two Conway tubes were floated and then lifted into position in March and October 1848; but it is a measure of Stephenson's greatness as an engineer that he did not allow that success to slacken his attention to the meticulous preparations for the launching and placing of the great Britannia tubes. He asked Brunel and Locke to join him in supervising the critical movements, and they did.

Thousands of people assembled to watch in silence the ticklish job when it was at last ready to be carried out on 19 June 1849; some were in grandstands and more on the shores. A capstan on one of the pontoons failed, and the attempt had to be postponed. But on the next day, though the breeze was strong, all went well, and the first tube was floated to its position and, after an anxious time when a shore capstan jammed and bystanders had to be called on to heave, secured just clear of high water. In the next few weeks it was slowly jacked up into its final position and secured there, to be followed in turn by the three other long tubes over the water crossing. Those on the land spans had been assembled on the shore directly beneath their final positions and were jacked straight up. The first line of railway was opened to traffic in March, the second in October 1850. The whole work had cost over £600,000.

The visitor to the peaceful Menai shore today can hardly conjure up any notion of that spot when it was the scene of bustling activity, with hundreds of men employed on a novel and momentous enterprise; but until 1970 the bridge spoke, perhaps more directly than any other of the great engineer's works, of its designer's strength and directness. Then the tubes were so severely damaged by a fire in the timber linings that they had to be dismantled; and today arched spans (the requirement for a 100ft clearance throughout having been withdrawn) have replaced the tubes. But the great towers are there; and it is still possible to feel in its presence some sense of the qualities that lifted this great bridge far above the ordinary and made it a symbol of the whole expansive, railway-building age which at its best could rise to a true nobility.

10
Robert Stephenson
in the fifties

◆

Years of such intense activity could not be passed without leaving their marks of severe strain on a constitution which though wiry was never really robust. In addition to the incessant responsibility and nervous anxiety, he had been physically much shaken in a collision on the Chester & Holyhead line at Conway in August 1848; and, after the completion of the Britannia Bridge in 1850, when he was forty-seven, his personal exertion slackened somewhat. He had no taste for retiring to the country to recuperate, but in 1850 he bought a yacht, the *Titania*. She and her successor, of the same name, were Robert Stephenson's 'house without a knocker', where he could secure the privacy that he so much desired but could not get at home. Yet even his sea trips led to more work: commissions first in Norway, then in Egypt, arose out of the cruises.

He was still engaged in a great string of works – at home, the Nene River improvement, the Norfolk estuary scheme, the Liverpool waterworks, and similar undertakings; abroad, on Norwegian and Egyptian railways and on the great tubular bridge over the St Lawrence at Montreal, later called the Victoria Bridge. This was a structure some 6,650 ft long, with twenty-five openings, the middle one (for navigation) being 330 ft wide, the rest over the river 242 ft, with a clearance above summer water level of 60 ft at the centre span. The special problem here, both in design and erection, was ice: the piers standing in the river had to be designed with upstream surfaces specially strengthened and shaped to withstand the ice floating downstream which could easily demolish and carry away any ordinary obstacle; and because of the frost no more than six months' work could be done in a year on the masonry of the piers. Stephenson twice visited Canada for the bridge, and he took responsibility for the design, but its execution was the work of A. M. Ross. The bridge was completed in 1859, after Stephenson's death, and the piers (though not the superstructures) remained as they were built until 1942, when they were reconstructed.

Robert Stephenson's connexion with Egypt was important, for he was responsible for designing the Alexandria–Cairo railway, with great swing-bridges at Benha and Birket-el-Saba, and also for confirming English beliefs that the Suez Canal was a wrong-headed project. He was the only English member of the original three-man survey committee of 1847, and he concluded that, while a canal could be constructed, it would be commercially unsound. The latest English biographer of Ferdinand de Lesseps observes that Stephenson received £55,000 in fees from the railway–'no small inducement in favour of rail against water!' The sneer is unjustified; there are attested cases of Stephenson, who had an ample income at this time, refusing valuable commissions, and it would be out of character for him, at the height of his fame and influence, to give anything but an honest view. When he repeated his opinion in the House of Commons in 1857, he associated himself with the speech against the scheme made by the Prime Minister, Palmerston, whom he followed in the debate; this gave Lesseps an opening to say that he had accused him of dishonesty and to issue a challenge. Stephenson must have thought the Frenchman absurdly touchy to think of appealing to sword or pistol on a difference of commercial judgement; he wrote a reasonable explanation, repeating his view but saying, which was true, that he had never impugned Lesseps' personal honour, and Lesseps had to be content with that. But Stephenson's misjudgement, which was shared by many other well-qualified people, helped to strengthen the British Government in its hostility to the canal, and he must be held partly responsible for the serious diplomatic reverse which the canal's triumphant opening in 1869 presented to British policy. Only Disraeli's *coup* of 1874, when Britain bought the bankrupt Khedive's shares in the canal company, went a long way to retrieve this setback.

In the 1850s Robert Stephenson lived a full and busy, though less anxious, life of public and professional commitments. He was elected Fellow of the Royal Society in 1849; was president of the Institution of Civil Engineers in 1856–8; received an honorary degree at Oxford University in 1857 (with I. K. Brunel and Dr Livingstone)–all the outward marks of recognition for a distinguished career. But he became melancholy, and sometimes even peevish, which he had rarely been before; he returned to visit his childhood haunts in the North-East and seemed to find pleasure in them (though he never became a bore, as his father did, on the subject of his early struggles). He read a great deal and built up a library; he bought a few choice paintings. He went to horse-races, but he never made a bet. But his work was done, and he knew it for some time before he died in his London home on 12 October 1859. Almost spontaneously it was decided that Westminster Abbey must be his burying-place, and 3,000 people filled the church. The driver of the first engine used on the construction of the London & Birmingham wrote to ask for a ticket, and was sent one. He was Henry Weatherburn, an employee of the South Eastern Railway with a good Tyneside name. So the story went back from the Abbey, through the mud of the railway works, to the Tyne, the collieries, and the wagon-ways from which the railway had been painfully born.

11
The imprint of the Stephensons

◆

George and Robert Stephenson left no direct descendants. George's only other child was a daughter Frances, who died when three weeks old in 1805, and Robert had no children. Robert's first cousin, George Robert, born in 1819, was the inheritor, under Robert's will (proved at nearly £400,000), of the family share in the locomotive-building firm and the Snibston collieries. (The Derbyshire interests had been sold out of the family in 1851.) G. R. Stephenson became managing partner of the works in 1859, associated with Joseph Pease, Edward's son. He retired in 1899, aged eighty, and died in 1905. During his time the firm stood among the leaders in its field, and it also branched out into marine engineering.

But by the end of the nineteenth century the Newcastle site had become intolerably cramped; the expanding business needed a completely new set of workshops on a new site. So in 1902 a large new works at Darlington was opened. The original site was taken over by R. W. Hawthorn, Leslie & Co ('Hawthorn' recalling an echo from George Stephenson's young days). This firm and Stephenson's were merged in 1937, and seven years later the Vulcan Foundry, of Newton-le-Willows, near Warrington in Lancashire (which Robert Stephenson had helped to establish in 1831), took a holding. In 1955 the English Electric group absorbed all these companies; and down to 1963 the lineal descendant of the Stephensons' engine-factory of 1823 was building diesel-electric locomotives for British and overseas railways.

Alton Grange near Coalville in Leicestershire and Tapton House near Chesterfield, George's last two homes, still stand; so do his birthplace at Wylam, now a National Trust property, and his cottage at West Moor, Killingworth. Robert's London houses in Bayswater have gone, but a tablet commemorates him on a new building at 34 Gloucester Square. A 'Stephenson Memorial' school and institute was built on the site of Robert's birthplace at Willington Quay, and a Stephenson Memorial Hall, in a fearsome Gothic style, was opened

59

in 1877 at Chesterfield. There are at least three statues of George–one close to the High Level Bridge at Newcastle; another in St George's Hall, Liverpool; and one formerly in the great hall of Euston station. Baron Marochetti did a bronze statue of Robert, and there is a bust by Wyon at Newcastle, said to be the truest likeness. There are good formal portraits of both at the Institution of Civil Engineers; the subject of a rougher, but perhaps more expressive, painting has recently been identified as George Stephenson, probably painted in his thirties. George's centenary in 1881 was elaborately celebrated at Newcastle; and in Rome, Italian railwaymen erected a plaque in his memory. A Hungarian postage stamp issued in 1948 carried his portrait and something looking like the *Rocket*.

Locomotion No. 1, the first Stockton & Darlington engine, is preserved at Darlington. The *Rocket* was much altered from its prize-winning form in 1831, and it remained at work until 1844. Several full-scale replicas from the first design were made (including one for Henry Ford), and one of these is now in the Science Museum, London, alongside the original rebuilt engine.

But the authentic stamp of the Stephensons is to be found not in these physical relics but in the imprint which they gave to railways over all the world: 'standard' gauge, general uniformity of practice, and the avoidance of specialized peculiarities which, though attractive locally, are of limited use–all in all, a strong, plain preference for what has been thoroughly tested and found practical. Some countries and some railways have chosen to ignore these lessons, usually with bad results; but not many. There was development but no revolution in the techniques of railway working for a century after George's death. New methods of traction–electric and diesel–were introduced in some places, often without their full potential value being obtained; but the basic conception of the railway remained unchanged. The Stephensonian framework appeared to be so firm that railways waited over-long before refashioning themselves to deal with a new kind of world, having other forms of transport in it, which is very different from the age of coal and iron in which they grew up. But some of the Stephensons' guiding principles–concern for stability and safety, an assured commercial basis, and the utmost freedom of interchange and through working of vehicles–must always be fundamental so long as there are railways.

So viewed, the Stephensons were great railway pioneers. Contributions were made by other men, many of them of high individual importance; but these two, beyond anyone else, grasped the principle of the railway as an organism, that is to say, that it was potentially something more than a collection of techniques which when applied together could be made to perform a useful job. They looked beyond that and had the vision to perceive the effects that quick and cheap land transport could produce; and they had the tenacity of spirit, allied to the practical ability, to translate the vision into workaday terms and so to release the immense forces for economic growth that were latent in Britain. Before the steam railway, production and expansion of distribution were being held back by slow, uncertain, and costly transport; the pack-horse, the coach, even the recently-built canals could never meet the pressing demands that the application of machinery to manufacture was already bringing forth in the 1820s. Lack of transport was like a padlock on a gate which prevented industry from expanding. Several people could see that the steam railway was the key to undo the padlock; the Stephensons turned the key.

Their contribution did as much as anything to produce the massive upswing of production in Britain between 1820 and 1850. In 1820 the annual output of iron–the basic industrial material–was about 400,000 tons; in 1850 it was more than five times as much. In 1820 something like 16 million tons of coal were mined and sold; in 1850, 56 million. Exports averaged £35 million a year in 1825–30, £61 million in 1845–50. The population of Britain was nearly 11 million in 1801, over 14 million in 1821, and 21 million in 1851. Industrial output and economic activity were rising at a rate never before considered possible. The railway had not done this unaided, but without the railway it could never have happened.

The railway also changed social life; indeed, it made a revolution. No part of the country remained inaccessible and remote, as many districts were in 1800; people began to travel in great numbers for business and to move about for work, holidays, weekends, even day trips, in a manner and in numbers hitherto inconceivable. Newspapers were delivered over hundreds of miles on the day of publication; fresh milk and fish began to be obtainable in cities which had known them only as luxuries; suburbs began to surround cities at some distance, connected by railway trains. Places hitherto far apart in time were brought unimaginably closer together: it took Sir Robert Peel fifteen days of hard travelling to reach London from Rome when he was required urgently to kiss hands as Prime Minister in 1834; twenty years later three days would suffice. Before the railway, Britain's society was based, economically speaking, on local, and mainly rural, interests; the railway transformed this loose community into a tightly-knit national economy which would be able to exert all its strength because of quick and cheap internal communications. It did the same, in varying degrees, for other countries too in their turn. It created the modern age. Without the Stephensons, something of the same kind would no doubt have happened; but it would hardly have come about as early, as economically, and as soundly as it actually did under the direction of their powerful and pervasive influence.

Bibliographical note

◆

The only sound modern account of the Stephensons is the full-length study by L. T. C. Rolt, *George and Robert Stephenson: the Railway Revolution* (Longmans, 1960). This is a lively and accurate work, though I have suggested different interpretations on some points. It includes a useful bibliography. Samuel Smiles's biography of George Stephenson was first published in 1857; the fullest and best edition is the fifth, of the next year. It was subsequently abridged and remodelled to include Robert, and it appeared in this form in *Lives of the Engineers* (vol. v of the 1874 edition). This was reprinted in a handsomely illustrated edition by the Folio Society in 1975. It remains valuable, though not all of Smiles's claims for George can still be accepted. Some of the anecdotes in Thomas Summerside, *George Stephenson* (Bemrose, [1878]) throw additional light. W. O. Skeat, *George Stephenson: the Engineer and his Letters* (Institution of Mechanical Engineers, 1973), is by no means a complete edition of the letters but a well-produced tribute to the Institution's founder.

J. C. Jeaffreson, *The Life of Robert Stephenson* (2 vols, Longmans, 1864), with engineering chapters by W. Pole, is detailed and useful. *Personal Recollections of the English Engineers* (Hodder and Stoughton, 1868) by 'A Civil Engineer' (i.e. F. R. Conder) gives an interesting sketch quoted on pages 43–4 of my text.

For the early development of railway construction, C. E. Lee, *The Evolution of Railways* (*Railway Gazette*, 2nd ed., 1943), is indispensable; see also M. J. T. Lewis, *Early Wooden Railways* (Batsford, 1970), and B. Baxter, *Stone Blocks and Iron Rails* (David & Charles, 1966). Much local detail is given by C. F. Dendy Marshall, *A History of British Railways down to the Year 1830* (Oxford University Press, 1938), though it must be added that much research and scattered publication in recent years has made some portions of the book out of date; for the North-East, W. W. Tomlinson, *The North Eastern Railway: its Rise and Development* (Andrew Reid, Newcastle-on-Tyne, [1914]). On the Stockton & Darlington, Tomlinson; J. S.

Jeans, *Jubilee Memorial of the Railway System* (Longmans, 1875); and K. Hoole's chapter in *Rail 150*, cited below. On the Liverpool & Manchester Railway, R. H. G. Thomas, *The Liverpool & Manchester Railway* (Batsford, 1980), supersedes all earlier histories of the enterprise, though two other works may also be consulted: R. E. Carlson, *The Liverpool & Manchester Railway Project 1821–1831* (David & Charles, 1969); and T. J. Donaghy, *Liverpool & Manchester Railway Operations 1831–1845* (David & Charles, 1972). For the Canterbury & Whitstable Railway, R. B. Fellows, *History of the Canterbury & Whitstable Railway* (J. A. Jennings, Canterbury, 1930).

On the growth of the British railway system, J. Simmons, *The Railways of Britain* (Routledge, 1961); for its effects on society and economic development, M. Robbins, *The Railway Age* (Routledge, 1962; Penguin ed., 1965); J. Simmons, *The Railway in England and Wales* (Leicester University Press, vol i, 1978; in progress); *Rail 150: the Stockton & Darlington Railway and what followed* (Eyre Methuen, 1975), ed. J. Simmons, including 'The Stockton & Darlington Railway' by K. Hoole. The relevant chapters in Sir John Clapham's great work, *An Economic History of Modern Britain* (3 vols, Cambridge University Press, 1926–38), are well worth reading.

On early locomotives, C. F. Dendy Marshall, *A History of Railway Locomotives down to the end of the Year 1831* (Locomotive Publishing Co., 1953); E. L. Ahrons, *The British Steam Railway Locomotive* (Locomotive Publishing Co, 1927, republished Ian Allan, 1961); for Robert Stephenson & Co, J. G. H. Warren, *A Century of Locomotive Building by Robert Stephenson & Co, 1823–1923* (Andrew Reid, Newcastle-on-Tyne, 1923). The history of *Rocket* is set out very thoroughly in B. Reed, *Locomotives in Profile*, vol i (Profile Publications, 1971), pp 149–72.

For further reading, G. Ottley, *A Bibliography of British Railway History* (Allen & Unwin, 1965).

Index

◆

Printed in England for Her Majesty's Stationery Office
by Billing and Sons Limited, Guildford, London, Oxford and Worcester
Dd 696356   K40